SO-BTE-329

Mathematics Lessons Learned from Across the World

Prekindergarten–Grade 8

Edited by
Johnny W. Lott and Carolyn J. Lott
Professors Emeriti
University of Montana, Missoula, Montana

NATIONAL COUNCIL OF
TEACHERS OF MATHEMATICS

more4u
www.nctm.org/more4u
Access code: LLW14574

Copyright © 2014 by
The National Council of Teachers of Mathematics, Inc.
1906 Association Drive, Reston, VA 20191-1502
(703) 620-9840; (800) 235-7566; www.nctm.org
All rights reserved

Library of Congress Cataloging-in-Publication Data

Lessons learned from across the world prekindergarten-grade 8 / edited by Johnny W.
Lott and Carolyn J. Lott, professors emeriti, University of Montana, Missoula, Montana.
    pages cm
  ISBN 978-0-87353-744-5
1. Mathematics--Study and teaching (Elementary)--Activity programs. 2. Mathematics-
-Study and teaching (Early childhood)--Activity programs. I. Lott, Johnny W., 1944-
editor. II. Lott, Carolyn J. (Carolyn Jernigan), 1944- editor.
  QA135.6.L465 2014
  372.7--dc23
                                    2014015894

The National Council of Teachers of Mathematics is the public voice of mathematics education,
supporting teachers to ensure equitable mathematics learning of the highest quality for all
students through vision, leadership, professional development, and research.

When forms, problems, and sample documents are included or are made available on
NCTM's website, their use is authorized for educational purposes by educators and non-
commercial or nonprofit entities that have purchased this book. Except for that use, permission to photocopy or use material electronically from *Mathematics Lessons Learned
from Across the World* must be obtained from www.copyright.com, or contact Copyright
Clearance Center, Inc. (CCC), 222 Rosewood Drive, Danvers, MA 01923, 978-750-8400.
CCC is a not-for-profit organization that provides licenses and registration for a variety
of users. Permission does not automatically extend to any items identified as reprinted by
permission of other publishers and copyright holders. Such items must be excluded unless
separate permissions are obtained. It will be the responsibility of the user to identify such
materials and obtain the permissions.

The publications of the National Council of Teachers of Mathematics present a variety of
viewpoints. The views expressed or implied in this publication, unless otherwise noted,
should not be interpreted as official positions of the Council.

Printed in the United States of America

Table of Contents

Introduction

This book is one of two designed to bring awareness to various international perspectives on mathematical topics taught throughout the world. Classroom activities herein showcase topics discussed at the International Congress on Mathematical Education (ICME–12) held in Seoul, South Korea, in July 2012.

ICME meets once every four years and is organized under the auspices of the International Commission on Mathematical Instruction (ICMI), an international body with representatives from around the world. The aim of ICME is to present current states and trends in mathematics education research and to examine current practices of mathematics teaching at all levels. Each ICME includes a wide range of participants, including mathematics education researchers, teacher trainers, practicing teachers, mathematicians, and others interested in mathematics education.

This book features activities for students ages five through thirteen, while the companion book features activities for students ages thirteen through eighteen. In collecting activities for the books, it became abundantly clear that different countries have different meanings and different ideas about what an "activity" is. These differences led to submitted activities being massaged into a truly international model that has remained primarily true to the original while infusing a degree of commonality for the purposes of these books. Classroom-tested activities were sought to exemplify some standard or guideline in different countries. Where possible, those standards are noted along with the *Common Core State Standards for Mathematics* in the United States.

The general features of an activity include the following: mathematical content; materials needed; setting the scene for the activity, including both country and classroom; teacher notes; extensions; research notes with references; and activity sheets. There are variations to these features depending on the age of students. We have tried to keep the country flavor of the activities by including native language in some instances, use of currency and measures of the country, and even symbolism and idiomatic language in others if the language was important in the country of the writers.

Research notes in the activities place the mathematics topics in an international setting with some sources in different languages. As editors, we have tried to make the research notes consistent throughout. What we found is that most activities can be located in a wider setting than a single country. What the user will see, however, is that activities for one country would never be used at the age or grade level given but might be used either earlier or later in other countries.

The activities presented are ordered by age level where they are used in the country and by content if there is more than one activity in a content area. Activity sheets are available for download at NCTM's More4U website (www.nctm.org/more4u). Check the title page in this book for your access code.

The audience for this book is classroom teachers, teacher educators, math coaches, elementary school mathematics specialists, and those who provide professional development.

In the selection process for the activities, we'd like to thank seventeen reviewers who worked with us. They made very important contributions to the activities themselves, as well as helping in the selection of the activities for the book. They are as follows:

Laura Bofferding, Purdue University, Lafayette, Indiana
Barbara Boschmans, Northern Arizona University, Flagstaff
Cindy Bryant, LearnBop, Missouri
Kelley E. Buchheister, University of South Carolina, Columbia
Mary Buck, Mathematics Consultant, Helena, Montana
Susan Gregson, University of Cincinnati, Cincinnati, Ohio
Jessica Taylor Ivy, Mississippi State University
Julie James, The University of Mississippi, Oxford
Catherine Halbur Lewis, retired, Silvis School District #34, Silvis, Illinois
Tom Lewis, retired, Moline, Illinois School District #40, Moline, Illinois
Woong Lim, Kennesaw State University, Kennesaw, Georgia
Anne Marie Marshall, Lehman College, Bronx, New York
Efia Mentuhotep, The University of Mississippi, Oxford
Giang-Nguyen T. Nguyen, University of West Florida, Pensacola
Alice Steimle, The University of Mississippi, Oxford
Cynthia E. Taylor, Millersville University of Pennsylvania, Millersville
Sue A. Womack, Utah Valley University, Orem

We'd also like to acknowledge the photography used in this book:
George Gibbs, weta; Susan Keall, tuatara; and Helen Taylor, kiwi

Chapter 1

A Witch's Different Soups: Mathematical Problem Solving, Number Concepts

Laurence Delacour
Malmö University
Sweden

MATH CONTENT

Number representations in addition

MATERIALS NEEDED

Items that students can find in a schoolyard or in a park or in the woods, such as rocks, sticks, pinecones, and so forth.

Tagboard and glue

Setting the Scene

Country of Context

In Sweden, children ages three to five spend a great deal of time outdoors during school hours. This allows teachers to work with mathematics in the schoolyard, in a park, in the woods, and so on. In Sweden, it is suggested that learning activities be presented in a playful manner.

Classroom Context

This activity is designed to take approximately an hour: one half hour to gather objects for use in creating number representations and another half hour of classroom time for documentation. More time may be required to get to any particular outdoor destination if the teacher wants to treat this as a mathematical field trip. Also, more time could be required depending on how much help the children need. Children can work in pairs or alone as the teacher chooses.

The activity allows children to explore different representations of ten or possibly higher numbers. If the children are already familiar with the concept of ten, the teacher may work with higher numbers.

Teacher Notes

The author suggests that the activity be presented as a fairy tale, beginning with the children sitting quietly in a circle as someone is coming to visit them soon. After a few minutes, another teacher, dressed as a witch, approaches the group. The visitor is very old and has difficulties walking. The children are told that the visitor, like all witches, has soup to eat every day, but now because of age, the children are asked to help to find ingredients to make the soup.

However, the visiting witch adds the following, "I am a very special and different witch. I want only ten ingredients, and no more than two different types of ingredients, in my soup, neither more nor less, and it'll just be pinecones and sticks (or whatever two ingredients the teacher knows the students can find). I do not want anything else in my soup. Just ten things and just the ingredients mentioned (for example, pinecones and sticks). Now will you help me by going in pairs and finding the ingredients I need to cook the soup?"

Each pair of students will find ten ingredients. For example, there will be combinations of pinecones and sticks, with a total of ten in each combination. Each pair of students should tell their classmates what ingredients they found and show the rest of the class their display of pinecones and sticks and tell how many of each they have. If the class agrees that this is a good combination, then these ingredients should be glued to the tag board in a row for display. (A tagboard illustration is modeled in fig. 1.1.)

A goal is to see that 10 could have many different representations such as 3 + 7 or 5 + 5. The teacher should try to have illustrations of all combinations that could represent 10.

When all combinations have been demonstrated, the children may draw a visual aid as in figure 1.1 showing the combinations. Learning becomes visible through the student documentation.

Extensions

An extension to this activity might be to find twelve ingredients necessary for another witch's soup.

The teacher may choose to use any higher number or to use more than two different types of ingredients.

Research Notes

If goals for early childhood education are defined in the curriculum and in a teacher's mind, then the teacher constructs both the decisive environment and experiences for children's learning and making sense of the world around them (Doverborg and Pramling Samuelsson 1999; Delacour 2013). The teacher must use personal knowledge to create situations, tasks, play milieus, and so forth, for students (Doverborg and Pramling Samuelsson 2011).

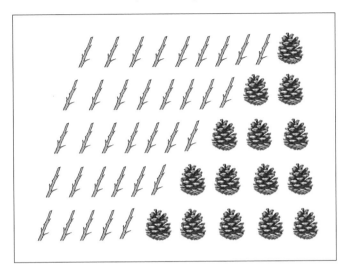

Fig. 1.1. Illustrations of representations of 10

In the *Common Core State Standards for Mathematics* (CCSSM) in the United States, under the kindergarten operations and algebraic thinking standards, students should "understand addition as putting together and adding to." For example, students "decompose numbers less than or equal to 10 into pairs in more than one way, e.g., by using objects or drawings, and record each decomposition by a drawing or equation" (National Governors Association Center for Best Practices [NGA Center] and Council of Chief State School Officers [CCSSO] 2010, p. 11).

REFERENCES

Delacour, Laurence. "Interpreting the Curriculum: Mathematics and Didactic Contracts in Swedish Preschools." *Utbildning & Lärande* 6 (February 2013): 64–78.

Doverborg, Elisabeth, and Ingrid Pramling Samuelsson. *Förskolebarn I Matematikens Värld*. Stockholm, Sweden: Liber, 1999.

Doverborg, Elisabeth, and Ingrid Pramling Samuelsson. "Early Mathematics in the Preschool Context." In *Educational Encounters: Nordic Studies in Early Childhood Didactics*, edited by Niklas Pramling and Ingrid Pramling Samuelsson, pp. 37–64. Dordrecht, the Netherlands: Springer, 2011.

National Governors Association Center for Best Practices and Council of Chief State School Officers (NGA Center and CCSSO). *Common Core State Standards for Mathematics*. Washington, D.C.: NGA Center and CCSSO, 2010. http://www.corestandards.org.

Chapter 2

Problem Solving with Basic Addition Facts

Cheng-Yong Poon
Kee-Jiar Yeo
Noor Azlan Ahmad Zanzali
Universiti Teknologi Malaysia

MATH CONTENT

Addition of sums up to 18

Combinations of two addends for the sum of 5

MATERIALS NEEDED

Egg trays

Table tennis balls

Activity sheet for each student

Colored pencils

Setting the Scene

Country of Context

George Polya's model of problem solving (Polya 1945) forms the basis for the problem-solving approach used in the Malaysian mathematics curriculum (Ministry of Education 2010). Teachers are required to help students solve problems based on this four-step approach.

- *Understand the problem:* Teacher guides students to understand and analyze a word problem. Specifically in Malaysia, students are guided to understand the meaning of the problem and the expected solution through teacher's demonstration and explanation.

- *Develop a plan:* Teacher discusses strategies students may use to solve a problem.

- *Implement the plan:* Students manipulate combinations of balls and record solutions on activity sheets.

- *Check the solution:* Students report solutions with verbal responses recorded on the blackboard. Teacher guides students to check and reflect on the solutions.

Listing possible cases systematically is one of the problem-solving strategies stated in the Malaysian mathematics curriculum (Ministry of Education 2010) to be taught in this activity. Although basic facts are procedural knowledge, the problem-solving activity enables students to learn conceptual knowledge and a problem-solving strategy if the task is open-ended and requires active thinking.

Classroom Context

This sixty-minute activity shows an example of teaching basic addition facts from the family of 5 commonly practiced by Malaysian teachers, especially in the mathematics remediation classroom or for students of ages five or six. Teaching methods involve a teacher demonstration with a story, possibly some individual work, and student group work.

Teacher Notes

The teacher may begin the lesson by using an experience from the students' daily lives in the form of a story. For example, the teacher may talk about a girl who is buying kuih (a type of local delight popular in Malaysia). It is sold in packs of five. There are two types of kuih: red bean and green bean. Customers may choose a total of five pieces of red bean kuih and green bean kuih to put into a plastic container when bought.

Using colored table-tennis balls and an egg tray, the teacher may demonstrate one of the possible combinations where the dark blue balls represent red bean kuih and the grey balls represent green bean kuih. For example, the teacher may arrange two dark blue balls and three grey balls on the egg tray as shown in figure 2.1.

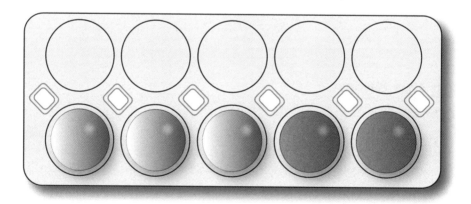

Fig. 2.1. Representation of 2 + 3 = 5

The teacher may record this representation with a related mathematical sentence as shown in table 2.1.

Table 2.1.
Recording sheet

Red Bean Kuih	Green Bean Kuih	Drawing of Beans	Mathematical Sentence
2	3	● ● ○ ○ ○	$2 + 3 = 5$

Students are asked to identify and illustrate the other possible combinations of the five pieces of kuih using the balls, that also give five pieces of kuih from combinations of red and green bean kuih and record the results.

After the initial trial, students may work in pairs or groups of three or four to discuss the way they arrange the balls in the tray and how they will list all the possible cases systematically.

The teacher may prompt the students to plan their strategy in manipulating the balls and recording the results. For example, they can list all the possible cases in a version of table 2.2 in a systematic way.

Table 2.2.
Systematic approach to finding all cases

Red Bean Kuih	Green Bean Kuih	Drawing of Beans	Mathematical Sentence
0			
1			
2			
3			
4			
5			

Extensions

After the students have completed the table of the 5 family, they might be encouraged to consider the family of 6 by recognizing that the numbers of red bean kuih are in ascending order while that of the green bean kuih are in descending order, but the total number in every case remains the same. This pattern also appears in the mathematical sentences. Students should be guided to reflect on the strategy they have used during the problem-solving process. They should justify the importance of using the "listing all possible cases systematically" strategy and when this strategy could be used to solve other problems.

The teacher may also ask students to identify and understand the mathematical properties among the basic addition facts such as the commutative, "plus zero" and "plus one" properties.

Research Notes

A mixture of two instructional approaches is applied in this activity. Initially, teachers demonstrate and explain an example based on the behaviorist framework of learning (Joyce, Weil, and Calhoun 2011). After that, based on the constructivist approach, students are required to use their thinking actively to plan the problem-solving strategy and make connections among a real situation and manipulative and abstract representations of a mathematical idea (Slavin 2009).

Also through this problem-solving activity, students may be guided to learn the mathematical properties for addition such as the commutative property and "plus zero" (Reys, Lindquist, Lambdin, and Smith 2007) to facilitate them mastering those facts.

In the *Common Core State Standards for Mathematics* in the United States, under the kindergarten operations and algebraic thinking standards, students should represent addition as putting together and adding to. For example, students "represent addition and subtraction with objects, fingers, mental images," drawings, sounds, "acting out situations, verbal explanations, expressions or equations" (National Governors Association Center for Best Practices [NGA Center] and Council of Chief State School Officers [CCSSO] 2010, p. 11).

REFERENCES

Joyce, Bruce R., Marcia Weil, and Emily Calhoun. *Models of Teaching.* Boston, Mass.: Pearson Education, 2011.

Ministry of Education. *Kurikulum Standard Sekolah Rendah: Matematik Tahun Satu.* Kuala Lumpur, Malaysia: Ministry of Education, 2010.

National Governors Association Center for Best Practices and Council of Chief State School Officers (NGA Center and CCSSO). *Common Core State Standards for Mathematics.* Washington, D.C.: NGA Center and CCSSO, 2010. http://www.corestandards.org.

Polya, George. How to *Solve It: A New Aspect of Mathematical Method.* Princeton, N.J.: Princeton University Press, 1945.

Reys, Robert E., Mary Montgomery Lindquist, Diana V. Lambdin, and Nancy L. Smith. *Helping Pupils Learn Mathematics.* New Jersey: John Wiley & Sons, 2007.

Slavin, Robert E. *Educational Psychology: Theory and Practice.* Upper Saddle River, N.J.: Pearson Education, 2009.

Activity Sheet

The table below may be used to record student work.

Red Bean Kuih	Green Bean Kuih	Drawing of Beans	Mathematical Sentence
0			
1			
2			
3			
4			
5			

Chapter 3

Basic Operations Activities

Nasim Asghari
Islamic Azad University, Central Tehran Branch
Iran

MATH CONTENT

Addition

Subtraction

Multiplication

MATERIALS NEEDED

Activity sheets for students

Overheads for teacher

Setting the Scene

Country of Context

These activities for primary grades ages six through nine were developed in Iran (Asghari 2010) and require only the operations of addition, subtraction, and multiplication.

Classroom Context

All activities are with full- and small-group discussion. The time for each task is approximately twenty minutes.

Teacher Notes

Task A

The teacher presents the class with the following problem: Sana is 2 years old and his brother Ali is 8 years old. When Sana is 5 years old, how old will Ali be? Students may use a table to represent the ages of the brothers. Upon completion, the teacher may ask volunteers to use their tables to present their solutions.

In question 2, the teacher will ask students to explain their solutions in their own words.

Task B

Students are given the following scenario: A mother frog and child frog stand at the end of a number walk. The mother frog jumps 2 spaces at a time. The child frog jumps 1 space at a time. The questions that students are asked deal with counting by 2s or looking at multiples of 2.

Task C

This activity has students add 20s and subtract 10s, depending on the symbol given. A smiley face adds 20 points to a score while a sad face decreases the score by 10. This activity is designed simply to give students practice adding and subtracting.

Task D

In this activity, students are asked to construct different numbers of airplanes and to determine the numbers of nut-screw combinations, pieces of wood, wheels, and tail fins needed. To construct one airplane, you need 10 nut-screw combinations, 8 pieces of wood, 3 wheels, and 1 tail fin. The students are asked to fill in the table and report any patterns they see.

Research Notes

According to *Principles and Standards for School Mathematics* (NCTM 2000), instructional programs in all grades should enable students to understand patterns, relations, and functions. Generalizing and formalizing patterns as relational thinking are important aspects of algebraic reasoning that can be addressed in the context of elementary students' work with arithmetic (Kaput 1998). Engaging students in relational thinking is important both because it can improve students' computational fluency (Koehler 2004) and because it promotes the viewing of expressions and equations as objects (Carpenter, Franke, and Levi 2003; Jacobs et al. 2007).

According to Iran's curriculum document (see website: www.talif.sch.ir, pp.126–28), students should represent and solve problems involving addition and subtraction and analyze patterns and relationships.

In the *Common Core State Standards for Mathematics* in the United States, the grades 1 and 2 standards state that students should represent and solve problems involving addition and subtraction (National Governors Association Center for Best Practices [NGA Center] and Council of Chief State School Officers [CCSSO] 2010, pp. 10, 15).

REFERENCES

Asghari, Nasim. "The Transition from Arithmetical Thinking to Algebraic Thinking in Curriculum of Iran: Designing a Model for Professional Development of Teachers Based on Early Algebra." PhD Diss., Islamic Azad University, 2010.

Carpenter, Thomas P., Megan Loef Franke, and Linda Levi. *Thinking Mathematically: Integrating Arithmetic and Algebra in the Elementary School.* Portsmouth, N.H.: Heinmann, 2003.

Jacobs, Victoria R., Megan Loef Franke, Thomas P. Carpenter, Linda Levi, and Dan Battey. "Professional Development Focused on Children's Algebraic Reasoning in Elementary School." *Journal for Research in Mathematics Education* 38, no. 3 (2007): 258–88.

Kaput, James J. "Transforming from an Engine of Inequity to an Engine of Mathematical Power by 'Algebrafying' the K–12 Curriculum." In *The Nature and Role of Algebra in the K–14 Curriculum: Proceedings of a National Symposium,* edited by National Council of Teachers of Mathematics and Mathematical Sciences Education Board. Washington, D.C.: National Academies Press, 1998.

Koehler, Julie L. "Learning to Think Relationally: Thinking Relationally to Learn." PhD Diss., University of Wisconsin–Madison, 2004.

National Council of Teachers of Mathematics (NCTM). *Principles and Standards for School Mathematics.* Reston, Va.: NCTM, 2000.

National Governors Association Center for Best Practices and Council of Chief State School Officers (NGA Center and CCSSO). *Common Core State Standards for Mathematics.* Washington, D.C.: NGA Center and CCSSO, 2010. http://www.corestandards.org.

Activity Sheet

Task A

1. Read the following problem: Sana is 2 years old, and his brother Ali is 8 years old. When Sana is 5 years old, how old will Ali be?

Use the table below to show the ages of the brothers and find the solution.

Sana's age	Ali's age

2. Is there ever a time when Ali will be exactly 3 years older than Sana? Explain your reasoning.

3. Explain whether there is ever a time when Ali will be exactly 10 years older than Sana.

4. Write a sentence showing the relation between Sana's and Ali's ages.

Activity Sheet

Task B

1. A mother frog and child frog stand at the end of a number walk. The mother frog jumps 2 spaces at a time. The child frog jumps 1 space at a time. If the mother frog makes 3 jumps, how many jumps will the child frog have to make to be on the same space with her?

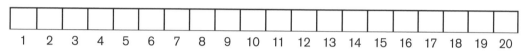

2. How many jumps must the small frog make to be in the same space as the mother frog when she has jumped 4 times, 5 times, 10 times?

3. Describe a relation between the number of jumps of the two frogs.

Task C

1. On the sheet below, you see the scores of three students, Farid, Farzam, and Amin. Each smiling face adds 20 to the student score and each sad face subtracts 10 from the score. What is the score of each student?

Suppose Ali has a score of 50. Draw a series of smiley and sad faces that would allow for this score. Explain why there may be more than one answer.

Task D

1. Construct different numbers of airplanes and determine the numbers of nut-screw combinations, pieces of wood, wheels, and tail fins needed. To construct one airplane, you need 10 nut-screw combinations, 8 pieces of wood, 3 wheels, and 1 tail fin.

Complete the table below.

	1 airplane	2 airplanes	3 airplanes	___ airplanes	___ airplanes
Nut–screw combinations	10		30		
Wood	8			32	
Wheels	3				15
Tail fins	1		3		
Total	22			88	

Explain whether it is possible to need 25 parts to build an airplane.

Chapter 4

Representation of Numbers by Place Value

Olimpia Rosa Castro Mora
Unit Measurement of Educational Quality, Ministry of Education
Peru

MATH CONTENT

Equivalent representations of the same number

Identifying different ways of decomposing a number by its place value

MATERIALS NEEDED

50 beans or pebbles

9 disposable cups per group of 4 students

Activity sheet for each student

Setting the Scene

Country of Context

Each year since 2007, a census evaluation has been applied to second graders in Peru to determine if students have developed the mathematical skills deemed appropriate for their grade. The results aid the Ministry of Education in helping teachers conduct classes to improve where needed.

In one of the latest censuses, the use of place value was assessed using questions about recognizing equivalences among different representations of whole numbers. A sample item is given in figure 2.1, showing egg cartons, each of which, when full, holds 10 eggs. (Note that in Peru, eggs bought by the 10s is not uncommon.) On this item, approximately 75 percent of the students did not recognize the equivalence of 46 and the response 3 tens and 16 units.

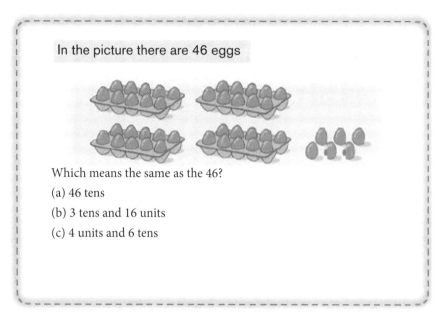

In the picture there are 46 eggs

Which means the same as the 46?

(a) 46 tens

(b) 3 tens and 16 units

(c) 4 units and 6 tens

Fig. 4.1. Ministry of Education Second Grade Census Item (Image is taken from http://www2.minedu.gob.pe/umc/ece2010/ECE2010Reportes/ Guiadeanalisis2doPruebadeMatematica_web.pdf, p. 23, Unit Measurement of Educational Quality.)

Classroom Context

The following activity (adapted from http://www2.minedu.gob.pe/umc/ece2010/ECE2010Re portes/Guiadeanalisis2doPruebadeMatematica_web.pdf, pp. 32–34) has been designed to help teachers work with students to help them identify different representations of the same number using different decompositions. The recommended classroom organization is for groups of four students.

Teacher Notes

Each group of students is given 9 glasses and 48 beans (although the number of beans is not mentioned to the students). The students are asked to place 10 beans in each glass and given time to do it.

Once this is done, students may be asked questions such as:

- How many glasses have been used?

- How many beans are left?

- Explain whether use of ten beans per glass and loose beans helps tell you how many beans there are totally.

In table 4.1, students are asked to use different media to represent this number and to express the total amount using addends from the representations. Table 4.1 on the activity sheet is blank, but is shown here with some possible representations. Note that these are labeled as in Peru with the terms "conventional forms" and "unconventional forms." For other users outside Peru, you may need to insert terms used locally.

Questions students might be asked when they are showing their work are the following:

- Can one use more than 4 glasses for 48? Why or why not?
- Can one use fewer than 4 glasses for 48? Why or why not?
- Explain why each representation is equivalent to 48.

Table 4.1.
Representations for 48

Representation Types	Conventional Forms	Unconventional Forms
Using glasses and beans		
Using tens and units	4 tens and 8 units	18 units and 3 tens
Using sums	40 + 8	30 + 18
Using board place value	Tens: 4, Units: 8	Tens: 3, Units: 18
Using graphics		
Using the abacus*		

*Note that the abacus is labeled using the Spanish abbreviations for hundreds, tens, and units.

Extensions

Perform the task using different two-digit whole numbers less than 50.

Research Notes

"Place value is an essential mathematical concept in the primary grades, and substantial research addresses children's emerging understanding of place value. In particular, Steffe and his colleagues (Steffe, Cobb, and von Glaserfeld 1988) have considered what it means for children's place value understandings to become more sophisticated" (Campbell 2002).

The *Common Core State Standards for Mathematics*, grade 1, standards say that students should understand place value and specifically "understand that the two digits of a two-digit number represent amounts of tens and ones" (National Governors Association Center for Best Practices [NGA Center] and Council of Chief State School Officers [CCSSO] 2010, p. 15).

REFERENCES

Campbell, Patricia F. "Connecting Instructional Practice to Student Thinking," In *Putting Research into Practice in the Elementary Grades: Readings from Journals of the National Council of Teachers of Mathematics,* edited by Donald L. Chambers, pp. 24–28. Reston, Va.: National Council of Teachers of Mathematics, 2002.

National Governors Association Center for Best Practices and Council of Chief State School Officers (NGA Center and CCSSO). *Common Core State Standards for Mathematics.* Washington, D.C.: NGA Center and CCSSO, 2010. http://www.corestandards.org.

Steffe, Leslie P., Paul Cobb, and Ernst von Glaserfeld. *Construction of Arithmetical Meanings and Strategies.* New York: Springer-Verlag, 1988.

Activity Sheet

1. Given 9 glasses and the set of beans, place 10 beans in each glass. Tell whether this can be done.

2. Fill in the table below as directed by your teacher.

Representation Types	Conventional Forms		Unconventional Forms	
Using glasses and beans				
Using tens and units				
Using sums				
Using board place value	Tens	Units	Tens	Units
Using graphics				
Using the abacus				

Chapter 5

Investigating Area

Christine Choquet
University of Nantes, CREN
France

MATH CONTENT

Preformula area concepts

Spatial visualization

MATERIALS NEEDED

String, thumbtacks, tagboard, and pencils (*Note:* some teachers may choose to use only pencils and paper for these tasks.)

Student activity sheet

Setting the Scene

Country of Context

The activity is used in primary school for students ages eight to nine in France. This is the fifth year in primary school (referred to as *cours moyen 2* in France), the last primary school level in France, just before middle school (referred to as *college* in France).

Classroom Context

The teacher may suggest that students work individually for a short time to think about task A and to begin to formulate an answer to the question about the area where the pet could go. Next the teacher may have the students work in small groups (three or four students) to produce a solution. Once all groups have arrived at solutions, each group may then be asked to explain its solution to the class, after which the solutions will be commented on and compared.

The organization above may also be used with task B. After both tasks are completed, the teacher may ask students for mathematical closure or propose a synthesis of strategies for solutions as well as working with students to determine the value of different solutions.

Teacher Notes

These tasks could be used for two purposes:

- Teaching pupils to organize their thoughts to resolve a geometry problem without teacher help

- Studying the notion of circle prior to a study of perimeter and area of a circle.

Task A

For task A, a pet is leashed to a post in such a way that the leash may revolve around the post. Mathematically this may be modeled with a point representing the post and a segment representing the leash. For young children, the teacher might have them try the problem using different lengths of string representing the leash. With older students, having them worry about the proportionality could be a challenge, since few will model this problem with an 8 m leash.

Task B

Task B expands on task A because the leash is attached to a wire. The leash is now 2 m long and the wire is 8 m long. This task will be much more difficult for some students and those students may truly need to construct a model to decide on a solution. Again for students with difficulties, starting without measures may be most helpful. Using a string representing the wire, the wire fixed to tagboard with thumbtacks, and a shorter string representing the leash may be helpful for these students.

The final drawing here might resemble a shape constructed as a rectangle with semicircles on each end. The purpose is the same then as task A: the potential shape to be drawn and the development of the ability to explain why the pet moves in this area. The abilities are linked to students' knowledge of circles, rectangle, and visualization.

Extensions

Based upon the intent of the original problem, there are many extensions that could be included. A teacher may propose other similar problems to promote searching and mathematical reasoning abilities at the students' level. For example, suppose the pet in task B is on the same length leash and the wire is the same length but is attached at both ends to a barn wall with the middle of the wire at the middle of a 30 m wall.

Research Notes

The intent of these tasks is to promote student knowledge using open-ended problem solving for students at this level (Arsac and Mante 2007; Artigue and Houdement 2007; and Choquet 2010). Additional work on visualization and perception in primary geometry has been written about by del Grande (1987).

In the *Common Core State Standards for Mathematics* in the United States, under the grade 2 (age eight) geometry standard, students should "recognize and draw shapes having specified attributes" (National Governors Association Center for Best Practices [NGA Center] and Council of Chief State School Officers [CCSSO] 2010, p. 20).

REFERENCES

Arsac, Gilbert, and Michael Mante. *Les Pratiques du Problème Ouvert.* Lyon: SCEREN-CRDP Académie de Lyon, 2007.

Artigue, Michèle, and Catherine Houdement. "Problem Solving in France: Didactic and Curricular Perspectives." *ZDM—The International Journal on Mathematics Education* 39 (August 2007): 365-82.

Choquet, Christine. "Problèmes Ouverts, au Cycle 3: Quelques Résultats sur les Choix de Professeurs des Écoles." *Actes du XXXVIIe colloque COPIRELEM*, ARPEME, 2010.

del Grande, John J. "Spatial Perception and Primary Geometry." In *Learning and Teaching Geometry, K–12,* 1987 Yearbook of the National Council of Teachers of Mathematics (NCTM), edited by Mary Montgomery Lindquist and Albert P. Shulte, pp. 126–35. Reston, VA: 1987.

National Governors Association Center for Best Practices and Council of Chief State School Officers (NGA Center and CCSSO). *Common Core State Standards for Mathematics.* Washington, D.C.: NGA Center and CCSSO, 2010. http://www.corestandards.org.

Activity Sheet

Task A

A pet is leashed to a post. The leash is 8 m long. Draw a picture of the area where the pet can move. In your drawing, show the post and at least one length of the leash.

Task B

A pet has a 2 m leash attached to a wire as shown below. The 8 m wire is shown with endpoints B and C. If the leash slides along the wire, draw a picture of the area where the pet can move. In your drawing, show the wire and at least three lengths of the leash.

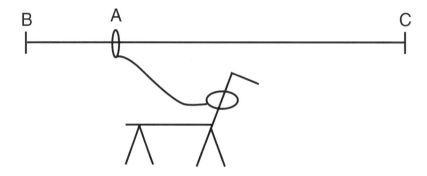

Chapter 6

What Are We Talking About?

Estela Vallejo Vargas
Pontifical Catholic University of Peru
Peru

MATH CONTENT

Division using partitions or distributions

MATERIALS NEEDED

Counters, up to 30 per person

Activity sheet for each student

Setting the Scene

Country of Context

In Peru, this activity may be used with students up to ages nine or ten. It may be done with students working individually or in pairs. Some teachers may have students who can do these tasks with little teacher intervention while some teachers may use the questions in the tasks as part of an introduction to division. *Equitable distribution* is used to mean each must receive the same number of objects, *maximum distribution* means that each must receive the greatest number of objects possible, and a *natural distribution* means that no object is cut into pieces to distribute it.

Classroom Context

Task A sets a scenario where students imagine distributing grains of corn to pigeons in a park. This scene may be simulated by using sheets of paper to represent pigeons and counters to represent grains of corn. The numbers vary according to the questions given in the task.

In task B, a teacher is distributing candies to students who participate in her class. If one followed the simulation as in task A, the pieces of paper would represent students, and the counters would represent the candies. In both tasks, students should be encouraged to write their answers to the questions both in math symbols and in words.

Teacher Notes

Task A

The teacher sets the activity in task A by telling students to imagine that they are on their way home after school. As they pass through a park, they encounter some pigeons. They should also imagine that they have grains of corn in their backpacks. The series of questions raised in task A may be considered by individual students or groups as the teacher chooses, but in task A it is very important that the work done in answering the questions be summarized for the entire class to see. Among the things the teacher may want to summarize is the language where the number of pigeons becomes the divisor and the number of grains becomes the dividend, and the number of grains left over after distribution is the remainder. The teacher may also choose to ask questions such as, "What are all the possible remainders when the divisor is 4?" or "What are the possible dividends when there is a 0 remainder?" The teacher may use divisor n (where n is a single digit) as either an extension or as a springboard for generalizations about divisions by single digits.

Task B

Task B is a scenario that has the teacher distributing candy to her class of 30 students. The series of questions asked on the activity sheet requires students to find all the divisors of 30 giving a 0 remainder.

Extensions

Children tend to benefit from making up their own oral or written stories that can be modeled by multiplication or division. Extensions of both task A and task B could involve having students make up those stories. For example, have the student make up a word problem that would match the number sentence $28 \div 4 = \square$.

Research Notes

Lampert (1989) wrote that children should be actively involved in devising algorithms in solving multiplication and division problems. Children should be able to explain what they are doing and demonstrate the validity of their algorithm by manipulating physical objects. Finally, children should be able to link symbolic representation to physical or pictorial representations.

In the *Common Core State Standards for Mathematics*, the grade 4 standards say that students should "find whole number quotients and remainders with up to four-digit dividends and one-digit divisors, using strategies based on place value, the properties of operations, and/or the relationship between multiplication and division" (National Governors Association Center for Best Practices [NGA Center] and Council of Chief State School Officers [CCSSO] 2010, p. 30).

REFERENCES

Lampert, Magdalene. "Research into Practice: Arithmetic as Problem Solving." *Arithmetic Teacher* 36 (March 1989): 34–36.

National Governors Association Center for Best Practices and Council of Chief State School Officers (NGA Center and CCSSO). *Common Core State Standards for Mathematics*. Washington, D.C.: NGA Center and CCSSO, 2010. http://www.corestandards.org.

Activity Sheet

Task A

While walking through a park on the way home after school, imagine that you encounter 4 pigeons. You remember that you have some grains of corn in your backpack from a science project. Answer the following questions about the distribution of the grains of corn to the pigeons.

1. Suppose that you have 12 grains of corn in your backpack.

    a. If all grains of corn are distributed to the 4 pigeons, how many does each pigeon receive?

    b. How many grains are left?

2. Suppose there are 13 grains of corn in your backpack.

    a. How many grains is each of the four pigeons going to receive after the distribution?

    b. How many grains are left?

    c. What if the number of grains is 14?

    d. What if the number of grains is 15?

    e. What if the number of grains is 16?

    f. What if the number of grains is 17?

3. Give different examples of numbers of grains of corn that could be distributed among the 4 pigeons with no grains left.

4. Give different examples of numbers of corn grains that could be distributed among the 4 pigeons with 1 grain left.

5. Give different examples of numbers of corn grains that could be distributed among the 4 pigeons with 2 grains left.

6. Give different examples of numbers of corn grains that could be distributed among the 4 pigeons with 3 grains left.

7. Give different examples of numbers of corn grains that could be distributed among the 4 pigeons with 4 grains left after distributions. Is it possible to give an example? Why?

8. What are the only possibilities of numbers of grains of corn that could be left after distributing different amounts among the 4 pigeons? Explain why there is no other possibility.

Activity Sheet

9. How many grains of corn will each pigeon receive if you have no grains in your backpack?

10. What if the next day you find 7 pigeons in your way home? How many grains of corn would be left after distributing equal numbers of grains among these 7 pigeons?

Task B

Imagine that Miss Clever, your mathematics teacher, has a bag of 30 candies for her class of 30 students. She wants to distribute all the candies only among the students in her class who participate in the class activity. Answer the following questions about that distribution.

1. Suppose that 4 students participated in Miss Clever's class.

   a. How many candies will each of these four students receive?

   b. Are there any remaining candies? If so, how many?

2. What if only 3 students participated in Miss Clever's math class?

   a. How many candies will each of these three students receive?

   b. Will there be any remaining candies? If so, how many?

3. If Peter is the only one who participated in Miss Clever's math class and the teacher keeps her promise, how many candies will Peter receive?

4. Give as many examples as you can of numbers of participating students in this math class so that Miss Clever could distribute the bag of 30 candies among these students and have no remaining candies.

5. What would happen with the distribution of candies if the numbers of participating students differ from the numbers you gave in number 4? Take into account that there are 30 students at most in the math class.

Chapter 7

Number Pyramids as a Mathematically Rich Learning Environment for All Students

Silke Ruwisch
Leuphana University Lueneburg

Torsten Fritzlar
University of Halle–Wittenberg
Germany

MATH CONTENT

Addition and subtraction of whole numbers with operative variations

Introduction to algebra

Pascal's triangle

MATERIALS NEEDED

Activity sheet for each student

Setting the Scene

Country of Context

In Germany, number pyramids, or number walls, may be used at many different levels for different purposes. This activity contains a collection of tasks that might be found in German textbooks and can be used for ages six through twelve.

Classroom Context

The activity is divided into tasks for different ages. These tasks may be done individually or investigated by groups of students. Wittmann and Müller (1990) describe a number pyramid or number wall in which students add the two numbers next to each other and write the sum in the stone directly above the two numbers. Typically the task format and special vocabulary is introduced to the whole group before children start to investigate special questions. Stones on the bottom layer of a pyramid are called base-stones while the top layer is the target-stone. Pyramids may be named by their height as well. For example, figure 7.1 shows different pyramids with a 2-pyramid on the left up to a 5-pyramid with five layers on the right.

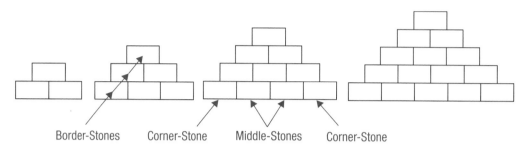

Border-Stones   Corner-Stone   Middle-Stones   Corner-Stone

Fig. 7.1. 2-, 3-, 4-, and 5-pyramids

To understand the principles of how number pyramids are built, how gaps can be filled in, or what effect the numbers on the base-stones have on the number on the target-stone, it is useful to look at a general number pyramid with algebraic notations as in figure 7.2.

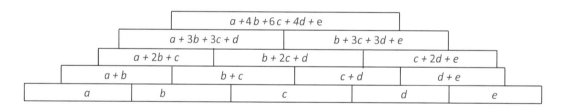

Fig. 7.2. Algebraic form of number pyramids

Note that the coefficients in each stone correspond to the numbers of Pascal's triangle or the coefficients of the binomial formula. More advanced students may use the algebraic structure to find the number entries of the stones.

Teacher Notes

Task A

In task A, children ages six or seven may practice addition and subtraction using either small number pyramids, as in number 1 on the activity sheet, or empty pyramids as in number 2.

Given empty pyramids as in number 2, students of all ages may build their own pyramids in a free invention setting (Hubacher and Hengartner 1999). Typical inventions use addition only.

Number 3 shows empty stones with numbers to the left that may be placed in those stones. These allow students to investigate the relations in a number pyramid. In trying to build a pyramid with all numbers given, they may recognize that the largest number has to always be placed on the top.

Number 4 allows students to create number pyramids with a given target stone of 20.

Task B

Number pyramids allow many different problem-solving activities, which can be worked on different levels, so that the same task may be used in heterogeneous groups of students or again for the same learning group in later years. For example, if a number pyramid has empty stones as in number 1, younger students may fill in the gap using a guess-and-check procedure.

Number 2 provides students with an opportunity to consider patterns and to construct a number pyramid using the found pattern.

For older students, more algebraic approaches to fill in the depicted gap in number 3 may also be used. For example, if the unknown number of the middle-stone is x, the numbers on the second layer can be represented by $31 + x$ and $6 + x$, and the equation $65 = 2x + 37$ for the target-stone number can be solved by using inverse operations.

Number 4 asks generalizations about the pyramids.

Extensions

The following extensions are found in different German texts.

1. Build pyramids with identical base-stones: Take three different numbers as base-stones of a 3-pyramid.

   a. Build all possible different number pyramids.

   b. Build the pyramid with the largest/smallest number on the target-stone.

2. Build pyramids with special base-stones:

   a. Investigate pyramids with the same numbers on the base-stones.

   b. Investigate pyramids with successive numbers (successive even numbers, successive Fibonacci numbers, etc.) on the base-stones.

3. Build pyramids with a given target-stone: Build (many, different, all) 3-pyramids with the target-stone 20 (100).

4. Build nested pyramids that need to be completed, such as the following:

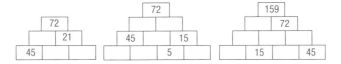

5. Complete pyramids with an underlying multiplicative relation between them.

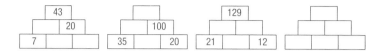

6. Build pyramids with gaps not filled in easily by adding or subtracting but which can be reduced to a 3-stones gap.

7. Build pyramids with systematic increase or decrease of base-stones and the consequences to the target-stone—

   a. Increase or decrease one corner- or middle-stone by 1 (2, 3, …).

   b. Increase or decrease every base-stone by 1 (2, 3, …).

8. Systematically increase or decrease target-stones and see the consequences to the base-stones. Build your own pyramid. Then, the number on the target-stone will be increased by 10.

   a. Can you find a solution by changing only one of your numbers on the base-stones?

   b. How many solutions can you find by changing two of your numbers on the base-stones?

9. Interchange the base-stones of pyramids—

   a. Interchange the numbers on the corner-stones. What do you notice? What happens to the target stone?

   b. Build a 4-pyramid. Then swap the numbers on the middle-stones. What do you notice?

   c. Swap two numbers on the base-stones. Which types of changes can you differentiate?

10. Compensate for changes. Build a 4-pyramid. The number on one middle-stone is increased or decreased by 1 (2, 3, …). Can you compensate for this change so that the number on the target-stone remains the same?

11. Verify statements: "If all numbers on the base-stones are the same, the numbers double in every layer."

Research Notes

Since the 1980s, problem-solving activities have become popular in Germany. Three lines of development led to activities like the one on number pyramids described here:

- Substantial learning environments (Wittmann 1998). In the view of mathematics education as a design science, the construction of substantial learning environments (SLEs), which are mathematically rich and designed around long-term curricula, are the heart of mathematics education.

- Investigation and exploration of situations (De Ponte 2007). Students' mathematical thinking is seen as being developed best by doing things the way mathematicians do. One of the main points is to investigate situations under a mathematical perspective (De Ponte 2007).

- Self-differentiation. If children deal with mathematically rich and substantial learning environments, the differentiation between children struggling with mathematics and those who are mathematically high achieving will emerge naturally (Wittmann and Müller 1990). The latter will develop a much deeper understanding, but all children are able to develop their mathematical thinking investigating SLEs.

This understanding of mathematics education is very popular in Germany and led to the construction of number pyramids as such an SLE (Wittmann and Müller 1990). Although younger children may need more guidance and preparatory work than older ones, they are seen as, treated as, and called "researchers," and most tasks are formulated as investigations with a lot of freedom in exploration (Krauthausen 2006). Besides this development of substantial learning environments, materials on how to introduce them are available to teachers with such learning environments and how to foster written and oral reflections (e.g., in the PIK-AS-Projekt to number pyramids—http://www.pikas.tu-dortmund.de/material-pik/ themenbezogene-individualisierung/haus-6-unterrichts-material/zahlenmauern-uebung sheft/zahlenmauern-uebungsheft.html).

In the *Common Core State Standards for Mathematics*, the grade 3, age nine, Operations and Algebraic Thinking 3.OA standard says that students should identify arithmetic patterns, and explain them using properties of operations (p. 23). The grade 6 standard Expressions and Equations says that students should be able to read, write, and evaluate expressions in which letters stand for numbers (National Governors Association Center for Best Practices [NGA Center] and Council of Chief State School Officers [CCSSO] 2010, p. 43).

Number pyramids could be a suitable instrument for bridging both standards and intertwining arithmetic and algebra because students can gather first experiences in dealing with unknowns in a motivating situation:

- They will be encouraged to use variables for representing relations between some stones of the pyramid (and possibly resulting linear equations could be solved by "backward calculations").

- They could establish relationships between unknown elements of the pyramid and use them for problem solving and discussion.

- Some students may be able to operate with unknowns as given numbers, which is very difficult for young students (Herscovics and Linchevski 1994).

REFERENCES

De Ponte, João. "Investigations and Explorations in the Mathematics Classroom." *ZDM—The International Journal on Mathematics Education* 39, no. 5–6 (2007): 419–30.

Herscovics, Nicolas, and Liora Linchevski. "A Cognitive Gap between Arithmetic and Algebra." *Educational Studies in Mathematics* 27, no. 1 (1994), 59–78.

Hubacher, Elisabeth, and Elmar Hengartner. "Kinder entwickeln vielfältige Aufgaben: Zahlenmauern (1. Klasse)." In *Mit Kindern lernen. Standorte und Denkwege im Mathematikunterricht,* edited by Hengartner, Elmar, pp. 69–71. Zug, Switzerland: Klett and Balmer, 1999.

Krauthausen, Günter. *Zahlenmauern. Zahlenforscher 1.* Donauwörth: Auer, 2006. CD-ROM und didaktische Handreichung.

National Governors Association Center for Best Practices and Council of Chief State School Officers (NGA Center and CCSSO). *Common Core State Standards for Mathematics.* Washington, D.C.: NGA Center and CCSSO, 2010. http://www.corestandards.org.

Wittmann, Erich Christian. "Mathematics Education as a 'Design Science.'" In *Mathematics Education as a Research Domain: A Search for Identity,* edited by Anna Sierpinska and Jeremy Kilpatrick, pp. 87–103. Boston and Dordrecht: Kluwer, 1998.

Wittmann, Erich Christian, and Gerhard Norbert Müller. *Handbuch produktiver Rechenübungen. Band 1: Vom Einspluseins zum Einmaleins.* Stuttgart, Germany: Klett, 1990.

Activity Sheet

Task A

1. Fill in the numbers into the pyramids.

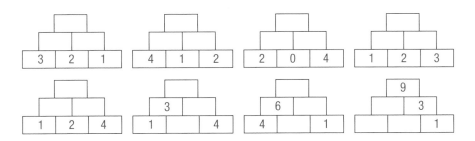

How did you find the appropriate numbers?

2. Create your own number pyramids.

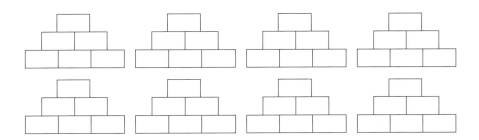

3. Fill in the numbers on the left into the pyramids on the right.

2, 4, 6
8, 10,
16

1, 2, 3
3, 5, 8

How did you find the appropriate place for the numbers? What did you notice?

4. Find number pyramids with the target stone 20.

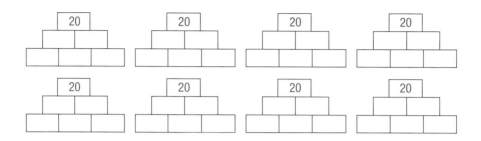

Describe how you found different number pyramids with 20 as the target stone.

Task B

1. Fill in the number pyramids!

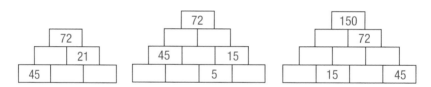

2. Fill in the number pyramids. What do you notice? Create a pyramid on the right using what you noticed.

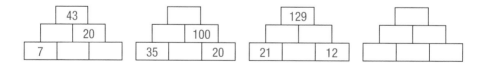

3. Fill in the number pyramid. Describe different ways of solution below the pyramid.

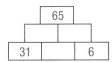

4. Fill in the number pyramid below.

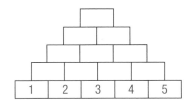

  a. How does the target-stone change, if you increase all base-stones by 1, 2, 3, ... ?

  b. Change one base-stone so that 60 results for the target-stone. How many solutions do you find?

  c. How does the target-stone change, if 2 (or 3) base-stones change their positions?

Chapter 8

Mr. Splash Provides Problems

Sharyn Livy
Mathematical Association of Victoria

Tracey Muir
University of Tasmania

Sandra Herbert
Deakin University
Australia

MATH CONTENT

Measurement with metric unit

Data collection and representation

Constructing data displays

MATERIALS NEEDED

Poster or digital pictures of Mr. Splash

Rulers (30 cm and 1 m), tape measures

Calculators (optional)

Butcher paper and markers

Tinkerplots (optional)

Setting the Scene

Country of Context

The Australian curriculum has four proficiency strands in mathematics: understanding, fluency, reasoning, and problem solving. These strands indicate the breadth of mathematical actions that teachers can emphasize. For example, within the strand of problem solving, the following description is provided:

Students develop the ability to make choices, interpret, formulate, model and investigate problem situations, and communicate solutions effectively. Students formulate and solve problems when they use mathematics to represent unfamiliar or meaningful situations, when they design investigations and plan their approaches, when they apply their existing strategies to seek solutions, and when they verify that their answers are reasonable. (Australian Curriculum Assessment and Reporting Authority 2012)

Classroom Context

This problem-solving activity is an example of a rich task suitable for students from ages eight to eleven. Within Australian primary mathematics classrooms, teachers regularly choose tasks such as these that are open ended and cater to a diverse range of learners. Such tasks have different entry points, allow for all students to succeed in finding a solution or range of solutions, and provide learning experiences that extend all students' mathematical understanding.

Students will work in small groups to measure their heights, arm spans, hand spans, and foot sizes.

Teacher Notes

The lesson may be introduced by showing a picture of Mr. Splash, as in figure 8.1.

Fig. 8.1. Mr. Splash

The teacher would then read the following: "This is a photograph of Mr. Splash. He loves to have a bath in his pajamas. He seems to be a bit big for the bath! I wonder how tall he is? How could we find out?"

Allowing students to brainstorm the problem of whether or not Mr. Splash will fit in the bathtub may bring the following suggestions:

- Measure the height of students in the class

- Measure the length of a bathtub and then estimate Mr. Splash's height

- Measure the size of students' hands and feet and then try and compare them to Sid and Mr. Splash

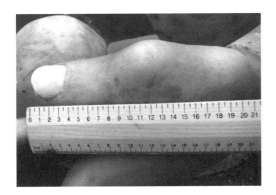

Fig. 8.2. Mr. Splash with Sid holding a meter stick

The teacher may next show the students a meter stick and draw attention to the meter stick in the photographs in figure 8.2. Based on the photographs, the teacher may ask students to predict Mr. Splash's height and to estimate their own height.

Measurement of body parts will continue with students working in small groups and completing the chart on the activity sheet. Of particular interest may be measuring consistency and measuring starting at zero. On the activity sheet, students will use measurements and make estimations about the measurements of Mr. Splash.

Extensions

Use the data collected on students to work out the average heights and lengths of students, including foot size.

Use the Australian Bureau of Statistics website (www.cas.abs.gov.au) to collect data from the "random sampler" to enable a comparison to be made with a larger sample size of similar-age students across Australia.

If the Tinkerplots software (Konold and Miller 2005) is available, students may investigate their collected data using Tinkerplots. A sample data entry table for Tinkerplots is seen in figure 8.3.

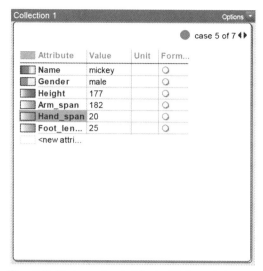

Fig. 8.3. Data entry table in Tinkerplots

Research Notes

"Zeroing is a common difficulty that students experience with many measuring devices. For example, students may be unable to use a ruler to measure length to the nearest centimeter, because they do not align the 0 of the ruler with one end of the object to be measured. This problem is exacerbated by the fact that 0 is often not right at the end of the ruler" (Department of Education and Early Childhood Development 2012).

In the *Common Core State Standards for Mathematics,* in grade 6 Statistics and Probability 6.SP, students summarize and describe numerical data sets by "reporting the number of observations, describing the nature of attributes under investigation, including how it was measured and its units of measurement," and describing any overall pattern (National Governors Association Center for Best Practices [NGA Center] and Council of Chief State School Officers [CCSSO] 2010, p. 45).

REFERENCES

Australian Curriculum Assessment and Reporting Authority. *The Australian Curriculum: Mathematics V4.2.* Sydney, Australia: Australian Curriculum, Assessment and Reporting Authority, 2012. http://www.australiancurriculum.edu.au/Mathematics/Curriculum/F-10.

Department of Education and Early Childhood Development. 2012. "Formal Units for Measuring: 2.25." East Melbourne, Victoria, Australia: State of Victoria Department of Education and Early Childhood Development, 2012. http://www.education.vic.gov.au/school/teachers/teachingresources/discipline/maths/continuum/Pages/formalunits225.aspx.

Konold, Clifford, and Craig Miller. *TinkerPlots: Dynamic Data Exploration.* [Computer software] Emeryville, Calif.: Key Curriculum Press, 2005.

National Governors Association Center for Best Practices and Council of Chief State School Officers (NGA Center and CCSSO). *Common Core State Standards for Mathematics.* Washington, D.C.: NGA Center and CCSSO, 2010. http://www.corestandards.org.

Activity Sheet

Below is a photograph of Mr. Splash. He loves to have a bath in his pajamas. He seems to be a bit big for the bath! How tall he is? How could we find out?

The following photographs of Sid holding a meter stick with Mr. Splash may be helpful in finding his height.

 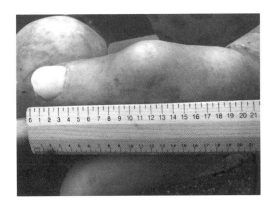

In your groups, measure your heights, arm spans, hand spans, and foot size. Record these measures in the following table.

Name	Height (cm)	Foot length (cm)	Arm span (cm)	Hand span (cm)

Consider the following questions.

1. Does the tallest person have the longest feet?

2. Does the tallest person have the greatest hand span?

3. Are hand spans and foot lengths related?

4. Are boys taller than girls?

5. Draw a representation of Mr. Splash on the butcher paper.

6. Estimate the following and explain your estimates:

    a. Mr. Splash's height

    b. Mr. Splash's height compared to the tallest person in class

    c. Mr. Splash's height compared to the tallest person in your family

    d. Mr. Splash's height compared to the tallest person in the world

7. Explain whether you think Mr. Splash has the dimensions of a real person.

Chapter 9

Who Will Win the Animal Race?

Te tauomaoma o ngākararehe
Robin Averill
Dayle Anderson
Victoria University of Wellington
New Zealand

Te Whare Wānanga o te Ūpoko o te Ika a Māui
Aotearoa New Zealand

MATH CONTENT

Generating simple number patterns from word patterns

Recording, comparing, and discussing simple number patterns

Representing simple number patterns with tables and graphs

MATERIALS NEEDED

Counters

1 cm by 1 cm grid paper

Rulers

Setting the Scene

Country of Context

The authors and the Ministry of Education in New Zealand conduct research related to culturally responsive mathematics education and equity of access to mathematics achievement. Students of ages eight to twelve may use this activity to study New Zealand animals while exploring and learning mathematical ideas. The authors acknowledge the work of

Pania Te Maro and Herewini Easton for their cultural and mathematical advice regarding this activity.

The problem-solving task was developed from the Ministry of Education activity Possum Poles (pp. 6, 7 and pp. 22, 23 respectively of *Figure It Out Algebra: Level 3* and *Answers and Teachers' Notes: Figure It Out Algebra: Level 3*). The Possum Poles activity and teacher notes are available online through www.nzmaths.co.nz. Further useful teaching ideas may be obtained from the Problem Solving and Algebra sections of the same website.

Classroom Context

This activity is designed to take up to three lessons. In the first lesson, students in pairs or small groups explore the comparison of three context-based number patterns. In the second lesson, students formalize their exploration using tables and graphs to record and represent the number patterns. In the third lesson, students in pairs or small groups create similar problems with number patterns for peers' exploration using a known context. The created problems will be checked for understandability and solvability, with refinements if necessary. The pairs/groups will then swap problems and use any known strategies for solutions, checking their answers with the problem creators.

Teacher Notes

Students are given the problem for each lesson with the teacher sharing the purpose of the lesson, checking that students understand what is required, and engaging students in a discussion about the problem. Students devise their own ways to explore problems without teacher intervention. Teachers may encourage students to consider whether tools or manipulatives would be useful for solutions. Teachers may support students unable to make progress on their own by suggesting they visit other groups. Depending on students' progress, teachers may need to plan leading questions.

Task A

The first task explores a race among three New Zealand animals: the kiwi, the weta, and the tuatara. In this race the first animal to go a distance of 16 km wins.

For a race of 16 km, the weta wins the race by reaching the finish line first. If the winner had been required to cross the finish line, the kiwi would have won.

Task B

The kiwi wins races of lengths 5, 9, 13, 17,. . . km as long as the winner is determined by reaching the finish line. The weta wins for races of all other lengths.

Task C

Students create tables showing the distance each animal has traveled each day. The information in the table is then depicted by showing the total distance covered by each animal per day in a graph.

Extensions

Students may be asked to make up a problem similar to the animal race problem using two or three different number patterns to define the moves. Follow the directions in tasks A through C and have other groups solve the problem.

Consideration could be given to the rate of each animal's movement as dictated by the pattern of their movements (e.g., 4 km/day versus 1 km/day) as well as to the distances traveled.

Attention may be paid to the Māori *whakatauki* (proverb) that says, "E kore te tauomaoma e riro tonu ana i te hunga tere, ko te pakanga rānei i te hunga kaha." ("The race is not always won by the swift, nor the battle by the strong.") The meaning of the proverb can be explored in relation to solving mathematical problems and carrying out mathematics investigations, how animals move and act, and to our lives in general. Students can also search for and share legends and other information about chosen animals.

Information about New Zealand animals can be found using the following links:

> http://kcc.org.nz/
> http://www.doc.govt.nz/conservation/native-animals/
> http://www.teara.govt.nz/

Research Notes

Students use a range of problem-solving strategies to explore the mathematics of a problem. For example, students could use manipulatives, solve a simpler problem, draw a diagram, act out a problem, or use tables and graphs for solutions. Carrying out the activity encourages students to consider and create suitable mathematical models for realistic situations while developing their understanding of recording and analyzing simple algebraic patterns. (See Hunter and Anthony 2010; Stein, et al. 2008; and Soares, Blanton, and Kaput 2006.)

In the *Common Core State Standards for Mathematics* in the United States, under the grade 5 (age 11) operations and algebraic thinking standards, students should "generate two numerical patterns using two given rules, identify apparent relationships between correspondence terms." Additionally, they should "form ordered pairs consisting of corresponding terms from the two patterns, and graph the ordered pairs on a coordinate plane" (National Governors Association Center for Best Practices [NGA Center] and Council of Chief State School Officers [CCSSO] 2010, p. 35).

REFERENCES

Hunter, Roberta, and Glenda Anthony. "Developing Mathematical Inquiry and Argumentation." In *Teaching Primary School Mathematics and Statistics: Evidence Based Practice,* edited by Robin Averill and Roger Harvey, pp. 197–206. Wellington, New Zealand: New Zealand Council for Educational Research, 2010.

National Governors Association Center for Best Practices and Council of Chief State School Officers (NGA Center and CCSSO). *Common Core State Standards for Mathematics.* Washington, D.C.: NGA Center and CCSSO, 2010. http://www.corestandards.org.

Stein, Mary Kay, Randi A. Engle, Margaret S. Smith, and Elizabeth K. Hughes. "Orchestrating Productive Mathematical Discussions: Five Practices for Helping Teachers Move beyond Show and Tell."

Mathematical Thinking and Learning 10 (April 2008): 313–40.

Soares, June, Maria L. Blanton, and James J. Kaput. "Thinking Algebraically across the Elementary School Curriculum." *Teaching Children Mathematics* 12 (January 2006): 228–35.

Activity Sheet

Who will win the animal race?
Te tauomaoma o ngā kararehe

There is a Māori *whakatauki* (proverb) that says: "E kore te tauomaoma e riro tonu ana i te hunga tere, ko te pakanga rānei i te hunga kaha," which may be translated as "The race is not always won by the swift, nor the battle by the strong."

In this activity you will be using number patterns to find out which animal will win a race.

Task A

This problem explores a race between three New Zealand animals, the kiwi, the weta, and the tuatara as pictured below:

| Kiwi | Tuatara | Weta |

For the race, each animal has a pattern to the way it can move. Your job is to find which animal will win by first reaching 16 km.

The kiwi moves 3 km one day, moves back 1 km the next day, and keeps repeating this pattern.

The tuatara moves 1 km each day.

The weta moves 4 km one day and stays put for three days, and then repeats this pattern.

Which animal wins the race?

How can you explain and justify why this animal wins?

Activity Sheet

Task B

Investigate whether the same animal always wins regardless of the length of the race.

What happens if the race is shorter than 16 km?

What happens if the race is longer than 16 km?

How can you explain and justify the answers to these questions?

In the problem, an animal wins by *reaching* the finish line. Are the race results different if the animal has to *cross* the line to win?

Are the movement patterns realistic for the animals?

If not, what is a more realistic pattern for each animal?

How can you show and explain your answers to these questions?

Activity Sheet

Task C

Construct a table showing the total distance each animal travels over a period of days. Use your table to present an argument about which animal wins the race.

Kiwi		Tuatara		Weta	
Number of day	Total distance from start	Number of day	Total distance from start	Number of day	Total distance from start

Use the information in the table above to create a single graph showing the progress of each animal. Use the graph to show what happens in the race.

Chapter 10

Making Pink-Rose Drink

Madihah Khalid
Nor Azura Hj Abdullah
Universiti Brunei Darussalam
Brunei

MATH CONTENT

Measurement of volume

Converting between measures

Multiply and divide compound quantities

Solve word problems

Use communication, connections, mental computation and estimation, visualization, and problem solving

MATERIALS NEEDED

Measuring cylinder

Water

Soda can filled with water

Red water (water mixed with red food coloring)

White water (water mixed with white food coloring)

Container that will hold about 2 L

Activity sheets for students

Poster paper or chart paper to record thinking and answers

Setting the Scene

Country of Context

Brunei has adopted English as the primary language of instruction. Thus, many students have to adapt to a new language while learning mathematics. Teachers of many classes in Brunei tend to be highly teacher centered, possibly as a result of students learning in a second language (Khalid 2008). However, more activities such as the one presented here allow flexibility in using groups for instruction as well as allowing more open-ended problems for class use. This activity is suitable for primary students ages eleven or older. The new Brunei Primary Mathematics Curriculum (CDD 2006) specifically mentions communication as one of the processes that need to be developed with the teaching of mathematical content.

Classroom Context

This sixty-minute activity allows for whole class instruction, group work in groups of four, and presentation time.

Teacher Notes

Task A

The first task is centered on the teacher talking to students about how to mix a drink for the class. Students then demonstrate how to measure and mix one version of the drink.

Task B

The teacher tells the entire class the following story:

Upin and Ipin are celebrating their birthday. They want to serve Opah's special pink-rose drink. So, Upin and Ipin asked for the recipe to make the drink. Opah listed the following items needed to make a jug of the drink:

- 1000 mL water

- 250 mL rose cordial syrup (or similar other flavored syrup available locally)

- 300 mL milk

- 260 mL soda

Upin and Ipin went to the grocery store and found the following:

- 1 bottle of mineral water is sold in a 1.5-L bottle

- 1 bottle of rose cordial is sold only in 1-liter bottles

- 1 1-L bottle of milk

- 1 can of soda contains 330 mL

The teacher asks the students to work in groups to help decide how much has to be bought to make five jugs of the drink. Additionally students are asked to record their thinking and answer on either poster paper or chart paper for sharing.

Answers may include the following:

- 4 bottles of mineral water

- 2 bottles of rose cordial

- 2 cartons of milk

- 4 cans of soda

A suggested rubric for assessing the posters and sharing the group work is given in table 10.1.

Table 10.1.
Suggested rubric for assessing posters

Level	Descriptors
4 Distinguished	• Shows complete understanding of a problem's mathematical concepts and procedures • Performs algorithms completely and correctly • Always uses appropriate mathematical notation (e.g., labels answers) • Identifies all relevant information and shows complete understanding • Selects a creative and efficient strategy for solving the problem • Shows clear evidence of a complete and systemic solution process • Gives an elaborate and effective explanation of the solution process • Succinctly explains "solution" to others • Uses precise mathematical language
3 Proficient	• Shows near complete understanding of a problem's mathematical concepts and procedures • Performs algorithms completely: computations may contain minor errors • Often uses appropriate mathematical notation • dentifies most relevant information and shows a general understanding • Selects an appropriate strategy for solving the problem • Shows some evidence of a systemic solution process • Gives an effective explanation of the solution process • Uses appropriate mathematical language
2 Apprentice	• Shows some understanding of a problem's mathematical concepts and procedures • Performs algorithms that may contain major computational errors • Seldom uses appropriate mathematical notation • Identifies some relevant information and shows limited understanding • Selects a strategy but unable to effectively arrive at a solution • Shows little evidence of a systemic solution process • Gives some explanation of the solution process but may be vague or difficult to interpret • Uses some mathematical language appropriately

Table 10.1. (continued)

Level	Descriptors
1 Novice	• Shows limited or no understanding of a problem's mathematical concepts or procedures • Performs algorithms that may contain major computational errors • Misuses or omits appropriate mathematical notation • Identifies little or no relevant information • Selects an inappropriate strategy for solving the problem • Shows no evidence of a systemic solution process • Gives minimal explanation of the solution process; may fail to explain or omits significant parts of the problem • Does not use mathematical language or uses it inappropriately

Extensions

This problem may be adapted with recipes from anywhere in the world. A different problem could be created by considering buying in local markets where more exact amounts can be purchased. Then a question of how much to buy may include fractional quantities not allowed when preexisting containers must be purchased. To do this, the teacher must be very aware of local buying and selling practices.

Research Notes

Communication is a mathematical practice that seems to be necessary in today's classrooms. Besides playing a role as an instrument for thinking mathematically, language is important for verbal representations, together with other representations such as diagrams, concrete materials, and symbols (Khalid 2008). In Brunei, some students are unwilling to speak in class as recognized by Martin (1996) when he said that apart from choral chanting, there is very little verbal output by students in Brunei classrooms. He added that when there is verbal output it is very often in the form of simple verbal recall statements. Salleh (2005) suggests that pupils in the Bruneian culture are not used to giving their views in a classroom setting. This activity is one of many now being tried to change the culture.

In the *Common Core State Standards for Mathematics*, the grade 4 (age 10) standards say that students should "use the four operations to solve word problems involving distances, intervals of time, liquid volumes, masses of objects, and money, including problems involving simple fractions or decimals, and problems that require expressing measurements given in a larger unit in terms of a smaller unit" (National Governors Association Center for Best Practices [NGA Center] and Council of Chief State School Officers [CCSSO] 2010, p. 31).

REFERENCES

Curriculum Department Darussalam (CDD). *Mathematics Syllabus for Lower and Upper Primary School*. Curriculum Department, Ministry of Education: Brunei Darussalam, 2006.

Khalid, Madihah. "Communication in Mathematics: The Role of Language and Its Consequences for English as Second Language Students," 2008. http://www.criced.tsukuba.ac.jp/math/apec/apec2008/papers/PDF/7.Madihah_Khalid_Brunei.pdf.

Martin, Peter W. "Code-Switching in the Primary Classroom: One Response to the Planned and Unplanned Language Environment in Brunei." *Journal of Multilingual and Multicultural Development* 17, no. 2–4 (1996): 128–44.

National Governors Association Center for Best Practices and Council of Chief State School Officers (NGA Center and CCSSO). *Common Core State Standards for Mathematics.* Washington, D.C.: NGA Center and CCSSO, 2010. http://www.corestandards.org.

Salleh, Romaizah. "Undesirable Academic Performance in Science: Is It Because of Language?" In *Proceedings of the Tenth Annual International Conference of the Sultan Hassanal Bolkiah Institute of Education,* edited by Harkirat Singh, Iorhemen John, Ogbonnaya Chukwo, Josage Sudharman, and Henry Quintus Perera, pp. 117–25. Osaka, Japan: The International Academic Forum, 2005.

Activity Sheet

Task A

Read the recipe for making the pink-rose drink; decide how to make any measurement conversions needed, and be prepared to demonstrate to the class how to make the drink in the empty jug.

Pink-Rose Drink Recipe

Ingredients

- 1000 mL water
- 250 mL red water
- 300 mL white water
- 260 mL soda

Supplies provided by teacher:

- 1.5 L bottle of water
- 1 L red water
- 1 L white water
- 1 can of soda water
- 1 empty jug

Task B

Upin and Ipin are celebrating their birthday. They want to serve Opah's special pink-rose drink. So, Upin and Ipin asked for the recipe to make the drink. Opah listed the following items needed to make a jug of the drink:

- 1000 mL water
- 250 mL rose cordial syrup (or similar other flavored syrup available locally)
- 300 mL milk
- 260 mL soda

Activity Sheet

Upin and Ipin went to the grocery store and found the following:

- 1 bottle of mineral water is sold in a 1.5-L bottle

- 1 bottle of rose cordial is sold only in 1-liter bottles

- 1 1-liter bottle of milk

- 1 can of soda contains 330 mL

Decide how much has to be bought to make 5 jugs of the drink.

Record your thinking and answers on either poster paper or chart paper for sharing.

Chapter 11

What Can We Learn from Natural Disasters to Prevent Loss of Life in the Future?

Soledad Estrella
Raimundo Olfos
Sergio Morales
Mathematics Institute
Pontificia Universidad Católica de Valparaiso
Chile

MATH CONTENT

Statistical representations

Graph comprehension

Decision making using mathematical modeling

MATERIALS NEEDED

Activity sheet for each student

Setting the Scene

Country of Context

This Chilean activity, designed for students of ages ten and eleven, deals with the tsunami that struck Dichato, Chile, on February 27, 2010. It was a result of the 8.8 magnitude earthquake occurring at 3:34 that morning. The normally tranquil beach town was hit by the tsunami about three hours after the earthquake. A major issue about when a warning could or should be issued resulted (http://www.globalpost.com/dispatch/chile/100304/dichato-tsunami-earthquake).

Classroom Context

For students who are aware of tsunamis, background on such occurrences may not be necessary, but for many who do not live near coasts, it will likely be necessary to have some whole-class discussion about the relation of earthquakes and tsunamis. Following this discussion, the teacher may want students to observe and reflect individually on the image on the activity sheet and the question, "What information do you see in the picture?" Next the teacher may ask that students share their thoughts in groups of twos or threes. Subsequently, work may be in groups and end with presentations and reflections on the students' work.

Teacher Notes

The teacher may show the image in figure 11.1 (also on the activity sheet) explaining, "I found this picture in a newspaper about the tsunami that hit the Chilean coast in 2010 after the 8.8 magnitude earthquake occurring that day at 3:34 a.m. The figure has information that can help save lives, so I am requesting that you help me organize the data in the simplest form so that it can be used as part of a warning system." Note that one issue is to determine the meaning of the numbers, 4:17, 5:50, and 5:20, above the arrow in the "water." Additionally, the meaning of the numbers, 11 m, 11 m, and 11 m, below Constitución must be determined. In the news report, the meaning is a wave of 11 m hit Constitución at 4:17 and another at 5:50 and another at 5:20.

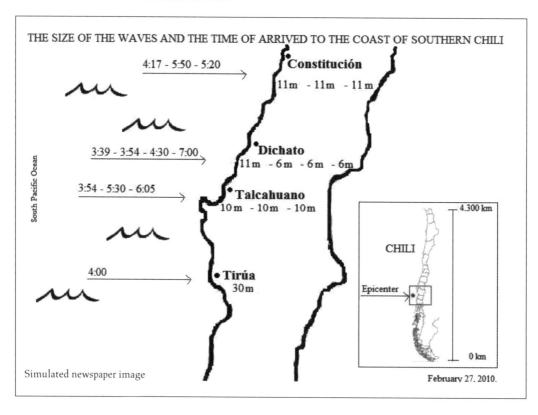

Fig. 11.1 The Size of the Waves and the Time of Arrival on the Coast of Southern Chile

The goal is to have students extract and organize information from the figure and decide how to communicate that information in a way that could help save lives in towns that might be affected by a tsunami.

Possible questions that the teacher may ask as either leading questions, when the students are determining information from the figure, or questions while students are making presentations include the following:

1. Do you understand the task?

2. What variables can you identify?

3. What types of life-saving messages might you want to send to different cities?

4. What type of information might you need to predict the number of waves per city?

5. How much time would be needed to give adequate warning to people on the coast between the times the earthquake occurs and the first wave hits the coast?

6. How can the information given in the figure allow you to predict time between waves if there is more than one?

7. What information do you think should be shared with people who live on the coast to provide the best warning message?

As a teacher, overarching questions for students to consider are the following:

The Size of the Waves and the Time of Arrival on the Coast of Southern Chile

1. Can lives be saved with what you have learned?

2. Are students able to "read beyond the data"?

Examples of what a teacher might want students to consider include the fact that in Chile, people died as a result of the tsunami because they returned to their homes, believing that the tsunami had only one wave; people also died because they went home believing that they had waited long enough. Tables 11.1 and 11.2 show information concerning the maximum time between waves and the number of waves from the newspaper article and the height of the waves in Dichato, respectively.

Table 11.1.
Cities, times between first and last waves, and number of waves

City	Time between the first and the last wave	Number of waves
Constitución	1 h 3 min	3
Dichato	3 h 21 min	4
Talcahuano	2 h 11 min	3
Tirúa	0	1

Table 11.2.
Waves hitting Dichato

City: Dichato		
Wave	Height (meters)	Time
1st	11	3:39
2nd	6	3:54
3rd	6	4:30
4th	6	7:00

Questions that the teacher might pose to students to get them to construct the type of message envisioned in the activity include the following:

- What variables such as height, place, and time do you see?

- How could you communicate a warning message to deliver to locations in Chile through graphics or tables?

Extensions

A possible extension would be to consider the warning time needed for the tsunami in Phuket, Thailand. Can you find comparable data to support your conclusions?

Research Notes

The tsunami activity is proposed to allow the student to conduct an exploratory data analysis, a la Tukey (1977): Students focus on the problem, plan how to solve it, extract data from the graphic image, analyze data through representations (graphs or tables), and communicate and compare the information with their peers. Moreover, the activity promotes development of higher-level graphical understanding (Curcio 1987; Estrella and Olfos 2012): students argue among themselves, and then the entire group discusses their final productions. Students seek relationships between quantities and apply simple mathematical methods to the data, so they understand the basic structure of the graph or table relationships developed as contained in such representations. In addition, students predict and infer about information that is implicitly present in the graphic context.

One of the mathematical practices in the *Common Core State Standards* at all grade levels is to model with mathematics: "Mathematically proficient students can apply the mathematics they know to solve problems arising in everyday life, society, and the work place" (National Governors Association Center for Best Practices [NGA Center] and Council of Chief State School Officers [CCSSO] 2010, p. 7). The tsunami activity provides the opportunity to students.

REFERENCES

Curcio, Frances R. "Comprehension of Mathematical Relationships Expressed in Graphs." *Journal for Research in Mathematics Education* 18 (November 1987): 382–93.

Estrella, Soledad, and Raimundo Olfos. "La taxonomía de comprensión gráfica de Curcio a través del gráfico de Minard: una clase en séptimo grado." *Revista Educación Matemática* 24 (August, 2012): 119–29.

National Governors Association Center for Best Practices and Council of Chief State School Officers (NGA Center and CCSSO). *Common Core State Standards for Mathematics.* Washington, D.C.: NGA Center and CCSSO, 2010. http://www.corestandards.org.

Tukey, John W. *Exploratory Data Analysis.* New York: Addison-Wesley, 1977.

Activity Sheet

The figure below is a newspaper image with information about the Chilean tsunami in 2010. Study the image carefully and answer the questions that follow.

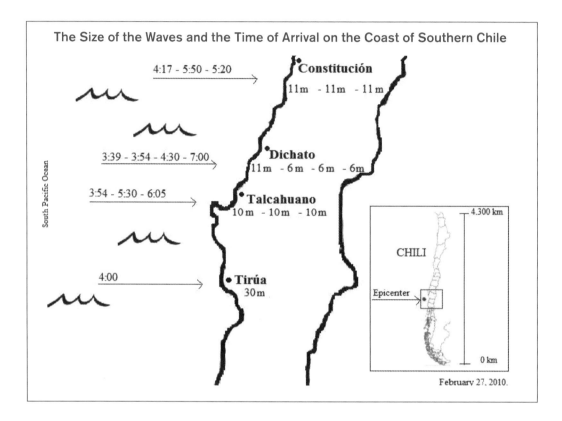

1. What types of information are given in the figure?

2. How much time would be needed to give adequate warning to people on the coast between the times the earthquake occurs and the first wave hits the coast?

3. How can the information given in the figure allow you to predict time between waves if there is more than one?

Chapter 12

Three Age-Changing Problem-Solving Activities

Hak Ping Tam
Yu-Jen Lu
National Taiwan Normal University
Taiwan

MATH CONTENT

Arithmetical reasoning

Proportional reasoning

MATERIALS NEEDED

Activity sheets with tasks A, B, and C

Spreadsheets (optional)

Setting the Scene

Country of Context

Mathematics lessons in Taiwan are traditional in that class exercises are usually centered on routine problems paralleling requirements of the national curriculum. However, at times teachers may provide open-ended problems that require a whole-class session. The intention of presenting these problems is to challenge learners with nonroutine problems to get the students to think deeply about the context of the problems rather than merely relying on identification of problem types. Tasks A, B, and C form a set of three problems that have been used with age twelve students. The problem-solving activities plus discussion are intended to take up the whole of a forty-minute class. The operations required in all three problems are within the reach of sixth-grade students (age twelve).

Classroom Context

The format for using the given tasks may vary according to the teacher's desires. However, task C likely will require more involved discussion among students. Thus, especially for task C, the use of either small groups of students or a teacher-led discussion may be needed.

Teacher Notes

The tasks are designed to be slightly vague in meaning, and so an immediate problem-solving technique for solutions may not be apparent. Students may need to give some serious thought about how to find solutions.

The solutions to these problems may require arithmetical reasoning plus a sense of proportional reasoning. By age twelve, many students will already have developed the habit of starting to compute whenever they encounter a problem rather than resorting to mathematical tools, such as making a table. As a result, there may be many wrong answers to problems, especially task C. The dynamical nature of age changes renders the making of a table very convenient for clarifying the relationship between the ages.

Task A

Likely, there may be several approaches to solving task A. A few students may claim that there will be no gifts since the age difference between the mother and son remains constant across the years. Most students may begin by listing the ages of both the mother and son in a table. Considering the listing or table, some students may notice that when the son is 7 years old, the mother will be 35 years old. Other students may use proportions to seek a solution to the task. At some point the teacher may want to ask students to discuss the meaning of "times" while they look for a relationship between the ages of the mother and son in the tables they made.

A more formal algebraic solution, which most students will not use, would say that if x is the age of the child, then the mother's age is $28 + x$. Thus you are seeking a solution to the equation $5x = 28 + x$ or the child's age of 7, making the mother 35. A more likely scenario for students is to construct a table using steps of one year and showing both the child's and the mother's ages.

Task B

Likewise, there may be several methods to finding a correct solution to task B. However, many students may have a mindset that age is always a discrete integer and may hence claim that no gift will be possible. The teacher may discuss with students if this is an unnecessary condition imposed on the task. In other words, fractional years can be considered.

An algebraic solution, which most students will not use, would say that if x is the age of the child, then the mother's age is $26 + x$. Thus you are seeking a solution to the equation $5x = 26 + x$ or the child's age of 6.5, making the mother 32.5. Or in a table, the steps this time will have to be 0.5 years. If the students chose to use one-year steps, as in task A, they will likely see that the solutions for the child's age is between 6 and 7.

Task C

The teacher may choose to treat task C as an extension of tasks A and B. Other teachers may simply treat it as a different task. It is expected that some students may use their experiences from solving tasks A and B in their approaches to task C. They may, for example, ask about the starting age of the mother. If the class has access to calculators or computers for this activity, the teacher may consider allowing them to explore a couple of starting ages of the mother using a spreadsheet.

In this task, because the mother's age is unknown when the child is born, one might expect more than one solution. If one thinks about this algebraically, using x as the child's age and y the mother's age when the child is born, then we are looking for a solution that is $5x = y + x$, or $4x = y$. Solutions to this equation will be found on the graph of the line, $y = 4x$. If the solutions sought are whole numbers, then the mother's age must be a multiple of 4 when the child is born.

The teacher may choose to encourage students to seek a reasonable strategy to find the relationship between the ages of the child and the mother rather than recording a long list of ages. Also, the teacher may encourage the students to pay attention to the context to check the reasonableness of their answers. If this is to be a real-life problem, then students should have a discussion at the possible real-life ages a female can be a mother.

Extensions

The tasks presented here may be extended into a more detailed mathematical modeling problem for older students.

Research Notes

Tasks A through C are structured activities, providing students an opportunity to discuss with one another and describe attempts at solutions. These tasks provide an opportunity for active teaching that focuses on meaning (Good, Grouws and Ebmeier 1983), as well as allowing students to construct the knowledge (Confrey 1987; Romberg and Carpenter 1986), necessary for successful and systematic approach to mathematical problem solving.

In the *Common Core State Standards for Mathematics* in the United States, the grade 6 Ratios and Proportional Relationships Standard says that students should "understand ratio concepts and use ratio reasoning to solve problems." Specifically, students should "use ratio and rate reasoning to solve real-world and mathematical problems, e.g., by reasoning about tables" or equations (National Governors Association Center for Best Practices [NGA Center] and Council of Chief State School Officers [CCSSO] 2010, p. 42).

REFERENCES

Confrey, Jere. "Mathematics Learning and Teaching." In *The Educator's Handbook: A Research Perspective*, edited by Virginia Richardson-Koehler, pp. 3–25. White Plains, N.Y.: Longman, 1987.

Good, Thomas L., Douglas A. Grouws, and Howard Ebmeier. *Active Mathematics Teaching*. New York: Longman, 1983.

National Governors Association Center for Best Practices and Council of Chief State School Officers (NGA Center and CCSSO). *Common Core State Standards for Mathematics.* Washington, D.C.: NGA Center and CCSSO, 2010. http://www.corestandards.org.

Romberg, Thomas A., and Thomas P. Carpenter. "Research on Teaching and Learning Mathematics: Two Disciplines of Scientific Inquiry." In *Handbook of Research on Teaching,* edited by Merlin C. Wittrock, pp. 850–73. New York: Macmillan, 1986.

Activity Sheet

Task A

Mrs. Chen was 28 years old when she gave birth to a son. She plans to give her child a large gift every time she is 5 times the age of her son. How many large gifts will the child receive from his mother? At what ages will he be when he receives the gifts? Please explain your answers.

Task B

Mrs. Lu gave birth to a son when she was 26 years old. She would like to present her child a large gift every time her age is 5 times the age of her son. How many large gifts will the child receive from Mrs. Lu? At what age will the child be when he receives the gifts? Please explain your answers.

Task C

Mrs. Lin gave birth to a son. She would like to present her child a large gift every time she is 5 times the age of her son. How many large gifts will this child receive from his mother?

Chapter 13

Figures with Equal Areas in Convex Quadrilaterals

Kiril Bankov
University of Sofia

Iliana Tsvetkova
Sofia High School of Mathematics
Bulgaria

MATH CONTENT

Areas of triangles with medians

Additive property of area

Convex quadrilaterals

Area of a quadrilateral using dissection into triangles

MATERIALS NEEDED

Activity sheet for each student

Rulers for prerequisite task

Setting the Scene

Country of Context

This is a Bulgarian activity for pupils eleven years old (Bankov and Iancheva 1992). According to the Bulgarian mathematics curriculum, pupils age eleven should know basic geometric shapes, such as triangles and quadrilaterals and their elements including median. Finding the area of a triangle is a major topic for this age. The basic problem of showing that a median divides a triangle into two triangles of equal area is common in Bulgarian textbooks.

Classroom Context

The authors suggest that in Bulgaria the work be done with teacher-student discussion throughout. The timeline is suggested as two consecutive academic classes of forty minutes each. For some classrooms in other countries, the basic problem mentioned above may have to be introduced and students will probably have to be allowed to experiment with the basic problem before going on. In these classrooms, the teacher may choose to devise an introductory activity for finding the areas of the subtriangles drawn when a median is constructed. A prerequisite requires students have knowledge of the formula for the area of a triangle ($A = ½$ base × height) and the concept of a median, a segment connecting a vertex of a triangle to the midpoint of the opposite side.

Teacher Notes

Prerequisite Task

A prerequisite task for this activity may include the following, and it is left for the teacher to determine the best method for teaching this prerequisite task:

Using triangle ABC below, construct $\overline{BH}$ perpendicular to $\overline{AC}$. $\overline{BH}$ is a height to the base $\overline{AC}$ in triangle ABC. If the length of $\overline{AC}$ is a and h is the length of $\overline{BH}$, what is the area of the triangle?

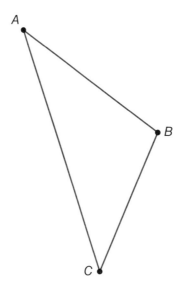

- In triangle ABC use a ruler to find the midpoint of $\overline{AC}$. Label that point D. Connect points B and D. The segment obtained, $\overline{BD}$, is a median of triangle ABC. What is the height of triangle ABD?

- What is the area of triangle ABD using the length a of $\overline{AC}$ and h? (Students should recognize that the area of triangle ABD is one-half the area of triangle ABC.)

- Similarly, what is the area of triangle BCD using the measures of triangle ABC?

Task A

To solve this problem, the teacher may need to ask, "Suppose M is the midpoint of $\overline{AD}$ and N is the midpoint of $\overline{DC}$. Are there ways to construct additional line segments in the figure to form triangles with medians?" (Diagonal $\overline{BD}$ is such a segment, giving triangle ADB with median $\overline{DM}$ and triangle BCD with median $\overline{BN}$.)

Task B

To solve this problem, the teacher may need to ask, "Is there a way to construct an additional line segment in the figure to form a triangle with a median?" (Diagonal $\overline{BD}$ is such a segment giving triangle ADB with median $\overline{BQ}$ and triangle BCD with median $\overline{BP}$.

Extensions

Problems 1 and 2 can be used as extensions of task A.

1. In the figure below, M, N, P, and Q are the midpoints of sides $\overline{AB}$, $\overline{BC}$, $\overline{CD}$, and $\overline{DA}$ respectively. Show that the area of the region shaded by dashes plus the area of the region shaded in blue equals the area of the quadrilateral $ABCD$. (Note that the central quadrilateral is shaded in both dashes and in blue; that is, its area is counted twice.)

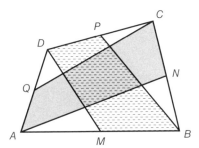

2. Use the figure below where M, N, P, and Q are midpoints of sides $\overline{AB}$, $\overline{BC}$, $\overline{CD}$, and $\overline{DA}$ respectively.

    a. Show that the area of the regions shaded by dashes is equal to the area of the regions shaded in blue.

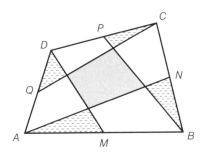

b. Show that the area of the regions shaded by dashes is equal to the area of the regions shaded in blue.

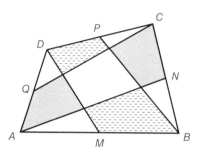

Problems 3, 4, and 5 can be used as extensions of task B.

3. In the figure below, M, N, and P are the midpoints of sides $\overline{BC}$, $\overline{CD}$, and $\overline{DA}$ respectively. Show that the area of the region shaded by dashes plus the area of the region shaded in blue equals the area of the quadrilateral $ABCD$. (Note that the central quadrilateral is shaded in both dashes and in blue; that is, its area is counted twice.)

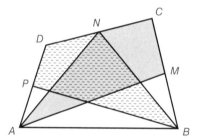

4. In the figures below, M, N, and P are the midpoints of sides $\overline{BC}$, $\overline{CD}$, and $\overline{DA}$ respectively. Show that in both figures (a and b) the area of the regions shaded by dashes is equal to the area of the regions shaded in blue.

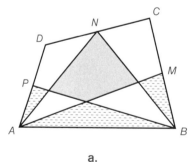

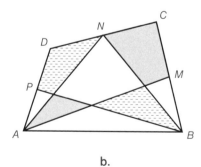

a.   b.

5. In the figures below, let M and N be the midpoints of sides $\overline{AB}$ and $\overline{CD}$ of the convex quadrilateral $ABCD$. In part a, show that the area of the region shaded by dashes plus the area of the region shaded in blue equals the area of the quadrilateral $ABCD$. (Note that the central quadrilateral is shaded in both dashes and in blue; that is, its area is counted twice.)

In part b, show that the area of the region shaded by dashes is equal to the area of the regions shaded in blue. (Note that the two triangles adjacent to side $\overline{AB}$ are shaded in both dashes and in blue.)

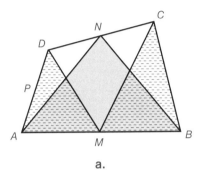

a.

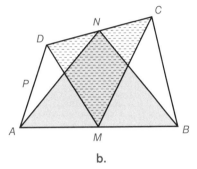

b.

Research Notes

This topic is found in most fifth grade (age eleven) textbooks in Bulgaria but is not usually taught at that age in the United States or Canada. Most classes in Bulgaria complete the prerequisite tasks (Bulgarian School Curriculum and Educational Programs, http://www.mon.bg/top_menu/general/educational_programs/). The extensions are usually proposed to classes with higher ability students, those with additional time for mathematics, or for extra-curricular work in preparation for mathematics competitions.

In the *Common Core State Standards for Mathematics* in the United States, the grade 6 (age twelve) geometry standard says students should be able to "find the area of right triangles, other triangles, special quadrilaterals, and polygons by composing into rectangles or decomposing into triangles and other shapes" (National Governors Association Center for Best Practices [NGA Center] and Council of Chief State School Officers [CCSSO] 2010, p. 44).

REFERENCES

Bankov, Kiril, and Jovka Iancheva. "Figures of Equal Area." *Mathematics & Informatics Quarterly* 2 (March 1992): 3–14.

National Governors Association Center for Best Practices and Council of Chief State School Officers (NGA Center and CCSSO). *Common Core State Standards for Mathematics*. Washington, D.C.: NGA Center and CCSSO, 2010. http://www.corestandards.org.

Activity Sheet

Prerequisite Task

Using triangle *ABC* below, construct $\overline{BH}$ perpendicular to $\overline{AC}$. $\overline{BH}$ is a height to the base $\overline{AC}$ in triangle ABC. If the length of $\overline{AC}$ is *a* and *h* is the length of $\overline{BH}$, what is the area of the triangle?

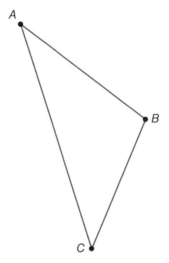

a. In triangle *ABC* use a ruler to find the midpoint of $\overline{AC}$. Label that point *D*. Connect points *B* and *D*. The segment obtained, $\overline{BD}$, is a median of triangle *ABC*. What is the height of triangle *ABD*?

b. What is the area of triangle *ABD* using the length *a* of $\overline{AC}$ and *h*? (Students should recognize that the area of triangle *ABD* is one-half the area of triangle *ABC*.)

c. Similarly, what is the area of triangle *BCD* using the measures of triangle *ABC*?

Task A

Recall that a median divides a triangle into two triangles of equal area. If *M* and *N* are the midpoints of $\overline{AB}$ and $\overline{CD}$ respectively, decide how to use this recalled information to show that the area of the shaded quadrilateral is one-half the area of quadrilateral *ABCD*.

Activity Sheet

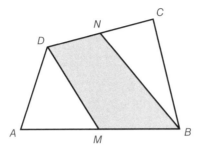

Task B

In the figure below, *P* and *Q* are midpoints of $\overline{CD}$ and $\overline{AD}$ respectively. Show that the shaded area is one-half the area of the entire quadrilateral *ABCD*.

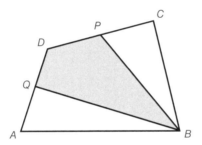

Chapter 14

Areas of Circles and Irregular Shapes

Mohamed Sayed Ahmed Abou
Ain Shams University
Egypt

MATH CONTENT

Area of circles

Areas of irregular objects

MATERIALS NEEDED

Student activity sheets

Rulers

Spreadsheet or calculators (optional)

Setting the Scene

Country of Context

In Egypt, task A is a problem in the sixth form primary, about age twelve (see Naser 2010). Finding the area of circles in a strictly problem format, as in task A, is common in Egypt. Task B is less common in schools.

Classroom Context

Task A is a traditional activity that could be an individual exercise or homework review problem.

Task B uses the area of a circle formula on an irregular shape. It uses notions of elementary statistics in approximating the area. This activity could be used for students of ages thirteen and fourteen working in small groups. It does require knowledge of the area of a circle formula. This activity will likely go better if calculators or spreadsheets are used for computations.

Teacher Notes

Task A

This task requires that students find the area of a given tabletop and, knowing the cost of glass, compute the cost of placing a piece of glass on the tabletop covering it.

Task B

Task B gives students an irregular shape and asks that they estimate its area. The first estimate may use any technique that the teacher wishes, including a grid, weighing, and so forth.

The second estimate uses an average (mean) of estimated areas where different lengths are used as radii. For an even better estimate than that found by small groups, the teacher may choose to combine all data found in the class. The teacher may choose to discuss the randomness of chosen "radii" in this process.

Extensions

An extension might be to allow students to use the technique in task B on known shapes like squares and triangles.

Research Notes

Evidence of finding areas in geometry is seen in the Rhind Mathematical Papyrus and shows that ancient Egyptians were versed in computing areas of some geometric shapes. For example, problem 48 compares the area of a circle approximated by an octagon with the area of a square circumscribing the circle. The result from this problem is used to find the area of a circular field (Clagett 1999).

In the *Common Core State Standards for Mathematics*, the grade 7 standards say that students should know the formulas for the area and circumference of a circle and use them to solve problems. Also students at this grade level should use data from a random sample to draw inferences about a population with an unknown characteristic of interest (National Governors Association Center for Best Practices [NGA Center] and Council of Chief State School Officers [CCSSO] 2010, p. 50).

REFERENCES

Clagett, Marshall. *Ancient Egyptian Science: A Source Book. Volume 3: Ancient Egyptian Mathematics. Memoirs of the American Philosophical Society 232*. Philadelphia: American Philosophical Society, 1999.

Naser, Mohamed Ahmed. *Mathematics for Sixth Form Primary, Second Term*. Cairo, Egypt: Ministry of Education, 2010.

National Governors Association Center for Best Practices and Council of Chief State School Officers (NGA Center and CCSSO). *Common Core State Standards for Mathematics*. Washington, D.C.: NGA Center and CCSSO, 2010. http://www.corestandards.org.

Activity Sheet

Task A

A table has a circular surface with diameter 1.5 m. The surface is to be completely covered by piece of glass. Calculate the cost if a square meter of the glass costs L.E 60 [60 Egyptian pounds]. (Approximate π as 22/7 or 3.14.)

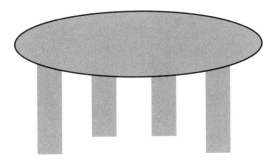

Task B

1. Estimate the area of the shape below.

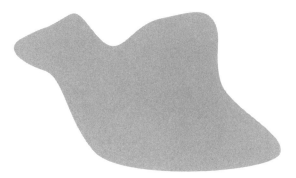

2. Pick a point in the interior of the shape above. Label it O.

3. Pick 10 points on the perimeter of the shape in number 1.

Activity Sheet

4. Measure and record the distance from O to each of these points in the table below.

Distance r from O to perimeter point	Approximated area of shape using value to left as radius and using $A = \pi r^2$

5. Use the measured distances in the table above as values for radii and estimate the area of the shape using $A = \pi r^2$. Record the estimated areas in the table as indicated in number 4.

6. Find the mean of the estimated areas in the table of number 4.

7. Explain whether the value found in number 6 is a reasonable estimate for the area. In your argument, use your original estimate of the area and any knowledge of data analysis.

Chapter 15

Taxicab Geometry: A Landscape of Investigation

Morten Blomhøj
Tinne Hoff Kjeldsen
Roskilde University
Denmark

MATH CONTENT

Measurement–distance

Mathematical reasoning

Mathematical representation

Problem solving

MATERIALS NEEDED

Activity sheet for each student

Setting the Scene

Country of Context

Children in Denmark begin schooling at the age of six in a comprehensive school covering grades 0–10, where grade 0 is an optional preschool class and grade 10 is an optional year for those who need one more year before beginning upper secondary education. In this school system, the mathematics curriculum includes inquiry-based activities as a regular form of teaching at all grades. These inquiry activities can take the form of small projects covering one or two weeks or the form of problem-solving activities covering one or two modules (90–180 minutes). In such activities, the emphasis is typically on the development of the students' competences in working with different forms of mathematical representations, in reasoning mathematically, in problem solving, in modeling, and in communicating in and with mathematics (in discussion, in written form, and through media).

Classroom Context

This inquiry-based activity is planned for ages ten to thirteen. This activity can help the students to develop productive beliefs about mathematics as a field for investigation, where they themselves can formulate interesting and relevant questions, where a basic concept such as *distance* can be given new meaning, and where their results and experiences can be organized based on their own reasoning.

Teacher Notes

Task A

One effective way of introducing the students to the activity is to present them with "a map of Square City" in the form of a squared blackboard or a transparency of a square grid. In Square City the streets form a uniform perpendicular lattice. Distance between intersections of streets (points) is measured by counting number of blocks (units) on one of the shortest paths following the streets between the two points, as in figure 15.1. For example, in figure 15.1 the distance between points A and B, denoted by $T(A, B)$ is 5 or $T(A, B) = 5$.

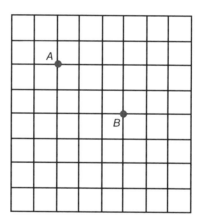

Fig. 15.1. Points *A* and *B* in Square City with taxi-distance 5 between them $T(A, B) = 5$

The teacher may ask the class: "What could we call a distance measured in this way in Square City?" Suggestions such as Square (City) distance, street distance, and road distance may arise, and a decision may be made by the class based on arguments and/or voting. Here, this distance measurement is called taxi-distance, based on "taxicab-geometry."

After having set the scene for the students' work in this manner, the students are presented with different tasks. The semi-real context of Square City makes it possible for the students to use their own language to make sense of the tasks and eventually to formulate their own questions in the context. "Why can we only measure distances between points of intersections between streets?," "People could be living in the centre of a square," "What if you have a helicopter; then is it possible to make shortcuts?" could be typical comments from the students.

A symbolic representation of the taxi-distance (or what the class has decided to call it) between two points *A* and *B* can be introduced as in figure 15.1: $T(A, B) = 5$. "To get from *A* to *B*, you need to go two blocks down and three blocks right. You can do this in whatever order you prefer, but there is no way to do it in less than 5 units, as long as you have to follow the streets. Therefore, the taxi-distance between *A* and *B* is 5 units."

With the scene set for the activity and the above introduction, the teacher may choose to continue leading the discussion or may choose to allow students to investigate on their own using the following about figure 15.1:

(A1) A round tour is one that starts and ends at the same point. A person is only allowed to change directions on a tour at intersections. If possible, draw round tours of lengths 4, 8, 9 and 12 beginning at point *A*.

(A2) If possible, find points that have the same taxi-distance to both *A* and *B*.

(A3) Suppose you change the position of *B* in figure 15.1 one unit in one of the four directions. How does that change your response to A2?

The dialogue between the teacher and the students during their tasks is important for helping the students to enter into a landscape of investigation (see research note). In an age thirteen class, a possible teacher (T), pupil (P) dialogue about A1 above follows:

P1: It is impossible to have an odd round tour.

T: Good; so what can be said about a round tour?

P2: It will have an even length.

T: Very good—nice to know, but can you prove it?

After some minutes the students may ask the teacher for help with the proof.

T: Each time you go one block north you have to go one block south somewhere on the tour, right?

P2: Yes, and the same with east and west.

T: Exactly. So if you go x blocks north and y blocks east, how can you express the length of a round tour?

Later, students may write the expression, $2x + 2y$, for the length of a round tour and argue that 2 times a number is even and that the sum of two even numbers is even, and that this proves the rule.

Students working with A2 will find no points with an equal taxi-distance to points *A* and *B* in figure 15.1. The teacher may lead a classroom dialogue to prove that it is impossible to find such a point in Square City. If there exists a point *P* with $T(P, A) = T(P, B)$, there will be a round tour *APBA* with the length $T(A, P) + T(P, B) + T(B, A) = 2T(P, A) + T(A, B) = 2T(P, A) + 5$, which is clearly an odd number. Since all round tours have even lengths, no such point can exist.

In this situation, students experience the power of a mathematical proof of impossibility in a context, which makes sense to them. Typically in a class, some students will try hard to find points with equal distance to point A and B in A2 before giving up and some will develop and discuss various arguments for why it is impossible to find such a point. All arguments should, of course, be presented and discussed in class.

Task B

The following, B1–B5, are investigated using figure 15.2.

(B1) Mark all the points that have the taxi-distance 3 to point A.

(B2) How many points did you find in B1? Suggest a suitable name for the pattern of points.

(B3) What happens if the distance is 4 or 5?

(B4) Build a formula for the number of points that have the taxi-distance r to A.

(B5) Build a formula for the number of points that have a taxi-distance less than r to A.

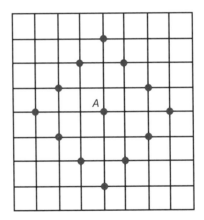

Fig. 15.2. 12 points with distance 3 to point A or a taxicab circle with radius 3

Depending on the age, symbolic representations may be introduced with reference to figure 15.2:

$N(r)$: Number of points in distance r to a given point—points on the taxi-circle.

$P(r)$: Number of points in distance less than r to a given point—points inside the taxi-circle.

By investigation (drawing and counting) students may develop a table similar to table 15.1:

Table 15.1.
*Number of points on ($N(r)$) and inside ($P(r)$) a taxi-circle
with radius* r

R	0	1	2	3	4
$N(r)$	1	4	8	12	16
$P(r)$	0	1	5	13	25

Students may investigate the pattern of table 15.1, and, with support from the teacher, formulate the recursive structure of $P(r)$. Some students will understand and express the relationship in their own words, such as: "The number of points within a circle of radius r must be the sum of the points within the circle of radius $r - 1$ and the number of points on the circle of radius $r - 1$." Yet other students may express their finding with symbolical representations such as: $N(r) = 4r$ for $r > 0$, and $N(0) = 1$; $P(r) = P(r - 1) + N(r - 1)$ for $r > 0$ and with $P(0) = 0$.

Given time and teacher support, students age thirteen may be able to find a closed expression $P(r) = 2r^2 - 2r + 1$ for the number of points inside a taxi-circle with radius r, either from geometrical reasoning or from working with the numbers in table 15.1, using a trial-and-error approach. At upper secondary level the formula can be deduced from the recursive expression.

Extensions

In the continuation of inquiry in this landscape of investigation, the students may pose interesting questions themselves based on their findings. A new system of tasks could be directed toward the combinatorial aspect of the number of different "shortest paths" between two given points, leading the students to the discovery of Pascal's triangle!

Another system of tasks could allow students to act as the mayor of the city. For example, given a city of a certain size and shape, where should three schools of equal size be placed to best cover the area? "What will be the average distance from a point in the city to the nearest school for solutions suggested by the students? What will be the maximum distance to the nearest school and how many points in the city will be at that distance to the nearest school? What criteria should be used to decide which solution to implement?"

Research Notes

Didactically, the activity refers to the concept of *a landscape of investigation* developed by Ole Skovsmose and explained by Alrø and Skovsmose (2002, pp. 46–67). A landscape of investigation in mathematics can have three different types of task contexts, namely a pure mathematical context, a semi-real context, or an authentic real context. Square City can be seen as a paradigmatic example of a landscape of investigation with a semi-real task context. This example of inquiry-based mathematics teaching is discussed further by Artigue and Blomhøj (2013).

In the *Common Core State Standards for Mathematics* in the United States, while there is no explicit use of taxicab geometry for the ages of students described here, the grade 8.F function has students "define, evaluate, and compare functions" and "use functions to model relationships between quantities" (National Governors Association Center for Best Practices [NGA Center] and Council of Chief State School Officers [CCSSO] 2010, p. 55).

REFERENCES

Alrø, Helle, and Ole Skovsmose. *Dialogue and Learning in Mathematics Education: Intention, Reflection, Critique.* Dordrecht, the Netherlands: Kluwer Academic Publishers, 2002.

Artigue, Michèle, and Morten Blomhøj. "Conceptualising Inquiry Based Education in Mathematics." *ZDM—The International Journal of Mathematical Education* 45, no. 6 (2013): 1–19.

National Governors Association Center for Best Practices and Council of Chief State School Officers (NGA Center and CCSSO). *Common Core State Standards for Mathematics.* Washington, D.C.: NGA Center and CCSSO, 2010. http://www.corestandards.org.

Activity Sheet

Task A

Below is a map of Square City. In Square City, the streets form a square grid. Distance between intersections of streets (points) is measured by counting the number of blocks (units) on one of the shortest paths following the streets between the two points. All travel must be along streets.

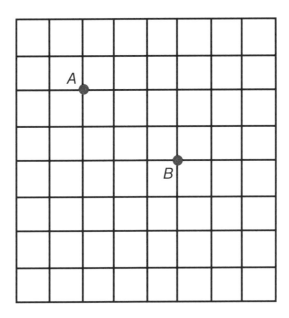

Map of Square City with points *A* and *B* marked

(A1) A round tour is one that starts and ends at the same point. A person is only allowed to change directions on a tour at intersections. If possible, draw round tours of lengths 4, 8, 9 and 12 beginning at point *A*.

(A2) If possible, find points, which have the same taxi-distance to both *A* and *B*.

(A3) Suppose you change the position of *B* in figure 15.1 one unit in one of the four directions. How does that change your response to A2?

Task B

Use the following map of Square City to investigate B1–B5.

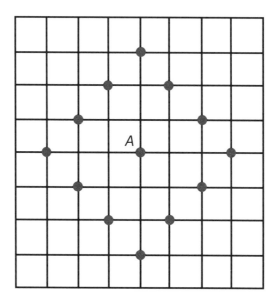

(B1)   Mark all the points that have the taxi-distance 3 to point *A*.

(B2)   How many points did you find in B1? Suggest a suitable name for the pattern of points.

(B3)   What happens if the distance is 4 or 5?

(B4)   Build a formula for the number of points that have the taxi-distance r to *A*.

(B5)   Build a formula for the number of points that have a taxi-distance less than r to *A*.

Chapter 16

Folding Paper as a Learning Resource

Rosa María García Méndez
Universidad Latina, Mexico City

Mariana Sáiz
Universidad Pedagógica Nacional, Mexico City
Mexico

MATH CONTENT

Properties of the angle bisectors in triangles

Finding the incenter of a triangle

MATERIALS NEEDED

Each student in the class should have—

• Three different triangles cut from colored paper

• Ruler

• Compass

Setting the Scene

Country of Context

The didactical approach and contents for mathematics education established in the Mexican National Curriculum for Basic Education (pre-K to ninth grades) are like those of other countries; the influence of the NCTM standards is manifest, and the concern about Mexican performance in global standardized tests induces these curricular similarities. From this perspective, the authors believe that the presented activities may be no different from those used in other countries.

The chosen activity was based on a textbook lesson that proposed to find the triangle incenter using ruler and compass. A teacher trying the lesson chose to use paper folding to carry out the exercise. The authors selected this activity because they observed that Mexican student teachers liked using paper folding to learn and to teach mathematics.

Classroom Context

This activity was developed by a Mexican mathematics teacher for children of age thirteen. The activity may be developed in a fifty-minute session; it is divided in two tasks, so that it can be used in two sessions if necessary. A prerequisite to the activity is student knowledge of angle bisectors, so it may be necessary to spend some time assessing the students' knowledge of angle bisectors. Teachers should encourage proper geometrical language for concept definitions and geometrical descriptions.

Teacher Notes

Task A

As a whole class activity, the teacher may ask students to take one of the paper triangles and determine how to find its angle bisectors without a protractor, a pencil, a ruler, or a compass. As the students' ideas are discussed, if they do not mention "folding paper," the teacher might propose it and let the students find out how to use this technique to accomplish the task as in figure 16.1. In figure 16.1a, triangle ABC is given. If $\overline{AB}$ is folded onto $\overline{BC}$, the fold line becomes line k making adjacent angles at vertex B congruent. Thus, line k is the angle bisector of angle ABC as in figure 16.1b.

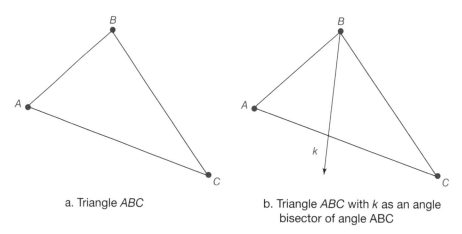

a. Triangle *ABC*

b. Triangle *ABC* with *k* as an angle bisector of angle ABC

Fig. 16.1. Folding an angle bisector of a triangle

When students understand how to find an angle bisector by folding the triangle, they might continue work in teams of three finding all three-angle bisectors of the triangle in each one of their triangles. With this task accomplished, students observe and analyze what occurs with the angle bisectors; that is, the three angle bisectors are concurrent. A summary of this task is the following: "The angle bisectors of a triangle are concurrent. The concurrence point is the incenter of the triangle."

Task B

In task B, students are asked to construct perpendiculars from a point to a line segment. In particular, students are asked to use their triangles from task A and paper fold the perpendiculars. An example is seen in figure 16.2b using the triangle in figure 16.2a. To obtain the desired perpendicular, find the fold line that contains point I and maps point C onto $\overline{AC}$. The fold line is the desired perpendicular.

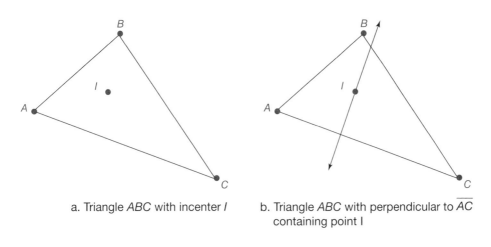

a. Triangle *ABC* with incenter *I*   b. Triangle *ABC* with perpendicular to $\overline{AC}$ containing point I

Fig. 16.2

Students should construct the perpendicular segments from the incenter, I, to each side of the triangle and measure them. They should conclude that in each triangle, the three measured distances are equal. If they use a compass and draw circles with center I and radius equal to the length of one of these segments, they should produce a circle inscribed in each triangle. If the teacher encourages them to discuss what they observe, an opportunity should arise to discuss terms like tangent and inscribed circle.

Extensions

As an extension, students may be encouraged to write a mathematical essay describing all work in the activity and using appropriate mathematical verbiage.

Research Notes

This activity is a level one or two in the Van Hiele model (van Hiele 2004), and it should not be taken as a proof of the angle bisectors concurrence. In the authors' experience, the concurrence of three lines or the alignment of three points are not surprising facts for students; they are not sensitive to perceiving the singularity of the situation. When a result of this kind is going to be presented, it is necessary that students are aware that the contrary is the common situation.

In geometry, students of all ages are likely to focus on noncritical attributes of geometrical examples; it is desirable that they change this tendency and overcome incomplete definitions and misconceptions. Hershkowitz (1990) states that one way to reach these goals is to provide a learning environment as rich as possible. So, folding paper and using origami and other material resources are all good approaches. These may be completed with more complex tasks and other resources such as geometrical software, but overall, encouraging children to justify or explain their thoughts and procedures must be a primary objective of mathematics education.

In the *Common Core State Standards for Mathematics* in the United States, the topics in this activity are normally not found until high school geometry. It does appear in Geometry—Circles (National Governors Association Center for Best Practices [NGA Center] and Council of Chief State School Officers [CCSSO] 2010, p. 77–78). One could extrapolate that this type of construction could be done in grade 8 under geometry 8.G where students understand that a two-dimensional figure is congruent to another if the second can be obtained from the first by reflection (NGA Center and CCSSO, p. 55).

REFERENCES

Hershkowitz, Rina. "Psychological Aspects of Learning Geometry." In *Math and Cognition: A Research Synthesis by the International Group for the Psychology of Mathematics Education,* edited by Pearla Nesher and Jeremy Kilpatrick, pp. 70–95. Cambridge, United Kingdom: Cambridge University Press, 1990.

National Governors Association Center for Best Practices and Council of Chief State School Officers (NGA Center and CCSSO). *Common Core State Standards for Mathematics.* Washington, D.C.: NGA Center and CCSSO, 2010. http://www.corestandards.org.

van Hiele, Pierre M. "The Child's Thought and Geometry" in *Classics in Mathematics Education Research,* edited by Thomas P. Carpenter, John A. Dossey, and Julie L. Koehler, pp. 60–66. Reston, Va.: National Council of Teachers of Mathematics, 2004. Originally published in 1959.

Activity Sheet

Task A

In this activity, you have three paper triangles to use. To illustrate the task, triangle *ABC* below is given, but you will use your paper triangles. The object in task A is to discover any relationship that you can find about the bisectors of angles *A*, *B*, and *C*.

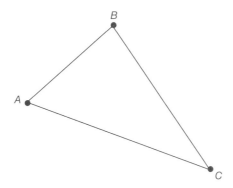

1. Paper fold the bisector of angle *A* by folding $\overline{AB}$ onto $\overline{AC}$.

2. Paper fold the bisector of angle *B* by folding $\overline{AB}$ onto $\overline{BC}$.

3. Paper fold the bisector of angle *C* by folding $\overline{AC}$ onto $\overline{BC}$.

4. What do you observe about the three constructed angle bisectors?

5. Complete these steps for each of your paper triangles.

6. Write a sentence describing your findings.

Task B

In task A, you found that the three angle bisectors of a triangle intersect in a single point. The angle bisectors are concurrent. The point of concurrency is the incenter of the triangle. Label it *I*.

1. Through point *I*, paper fold a perpendicular line segment to $\overline{AB}$ by folding point *A* onto $\overline{AB}$. Label the point of intersection of the perpendicular and $\overline{AB}$ as point *D*.

2. Through point *I*, paper fold a perpendicular line segment to $\overline{BC}$ by folding point *B* onto $\overline{BC}$. Label the point of intersection of the perpendicular and $\overline{BC}$ as point *E*.

3. Through point *I*, paper fold a perpendicular line segment to $\overline{AC}$ by folding point *A* onto $\overline{AC}$. Label the point of intersection of the perpendicular and $\overline{AC}$ as point *F*.

4. Measure each of the perpendicular segments: $\overline{ID}$, $\overline{IE}$, and $\overline{IF}$.

Activity Sheet

5. What conclusion did you reach in number 4?

6. If *I* were the center of a circle with radius *ID*, what points would the circle contain?

7. The circle described in number 6 is the incircle of triangle *ABC*. Triangle *ABC* circumscribes the incircle. Discuss with your teacher the relation of the incircle and the sides of the triangle.

Chapter 17

The Signpost: Where Was This Photograph Taken?

Doug Clarke
Anne Roche
Australian Catholic University (Melbourne Campus)
Australia

MATH CONTENT

Measurement

Map reading

Scaling

MATERIALS NEEDED

Atlases or maps of the world with appropriate scales

Rulers

A map of the Pacific Region (see fig. 17.2 below)

Mathematical compasses

Activity Sheet for each student

Setting the Scene

Country of Context

This activity was developed for students of ages eleven to fourteen in Australia, but a signpost photograph can be used from any country. The mathematical content will work for any location.

Fig. 17.1. Photo of distance map taken in a mystery city

Here the activity is built around airline distances but interested teachers could adapt this to railroad distances or automobile distances in more local contexts.

Classroom Context

It is suggested the teacher show the student activity page with the photograph (fig. 17.1) to the entire class and challenge them to work in pairs to decide where the photo might have been taken. Before students start work, they may discuss intended approaches to the problem and any early thoughts on the signpost's location. With the teacher moving around the classroom, students may be probed to explain their reasoning and may be observed to determine their use of scale and careful measurement. As conclusions are shared, it may be fruitful to have whole-group discussions of findings to explore different strategies and reasoning used.

Teacher Notes

For students who have difficulty starting the activity, one helpful prompt is to suggest that they pick one city named on the sign and then try to locate particular cities on the map which might be this distance from the signpost.

When this activity was tried in Australia, some students quickly chose Sydney and Fiji as the best places to consider because they noticed these were the closest and had similar distances from the mystery city. They were aware that the mystery city was an equal distance from Sydney and Fiji so their estimations now were more likely to be in the ball park.

Difficulties arose around the need to be accurate when converting and measuring, particularly when working with greater distances. Using a particular map of the South Pacific region and the corresponding scale, one pair of students determined that the mystery city was close to 5 cm from Fiji on the map, as in figure 17.2.

Fig. 17.2. Student circles used to guess the mystery city

The pair illustrated their insight by rotating a ruler around Fiji, and noting where 5 cm from Fiji "reached"; they knew that the city must be somewhere along this circle.

The teacher in the trial class took this opportunity to share the pair's insight with the class and introduced a compass to make the measurements more accurate. The student insight, along with the tools, led other students to realize that drawing the same-sized circle around Sydney would provide other useful information. Given the choice of two locations (the northern and southern intersections of the two circles), the students concluded that the mystery city was likely to be in New Zealand. Some students concluded this because there did not appear to be any cities (or land) at the northern point of intersection. Others calculated the distance from a third city (say Tahiti) to more clearly specify the location. In reality, the photograph was taken at Auckland Airport, New Zealand.

Extensions

Subsequent lessons might encourage students in groups to create their own signposts with cities of their own choices and then to pose their problems to another group.

Research Notes

Map scale is a very difficult topic to teach and to learn. Teachers may decide to do some introductory work on scale, but our experience is that "throwing students in the deep end" works well, as even if they do not completely solve the problem, much is learned about scale, different map projections, and the locations of various cities around the world (Clarke and Roche 2009; Sullivan, Clarke, and Clarke 2013).

A mathematical practice for all age students in the *Common Core State Standards for Mathematics* is to "make sense of problems and persevere in solving them" (National Governors Association Center for Best Practices [NGA Center] and Council of Chief State School Officers [CCSSO] 2010, p. 6). The map activity described uses ideas of ratios and modeling in geometry for solution.

REFERENCES

Clarke, Doug M., and Anne Roche. "Using Mathematical Tasks Built Around 'Real' Contexts: Opportunities and Challenges for Teachers and Students." *Australian Primary Mathematics Classroom* 14, no. 2 (2009): 24–31.

National Governors Association Center for Best Practices and Council of Chief State School Officers (NGA Center and CCSSO). *Common Core State Standards for Mathematics.* Washington, D.C.: NGA Center and CCSSO, 2010. http://www.corestandards.org.

Sullivan, Peter, Doug M. Clarke, and Barbara A. Clarke. *Teaching with Tasks for Effective Mathematics Learning.* New York: Springer, 2013.

Activity Sheet

The photo of a signpost below was taken at a city airport.

1. In which city do you think this photo was taken?

2. Explain how you worked it out.

Chapter 18

There Is Trouble in Paradise: Severe Water Shortage Problem in Cyprus

Nicholas Mousoulides
Constantinos Christou
University of Cyprus
Cyprus

MATH CONTENT

Linear equations

Measurement

Statistical concepts of means, weighting, range

Math modeling

MATERIALS NEEDED

Student activity sheets

Google Earth

Spreadsheet software

Setting the Scene

Country of Context

Water shortage in Cyprus is among the country's most important problems. This same problem is common in much of the world. Half of the planet's population is expected to face an insufficient water supply by 2025. Cyprus is increasingly relying on desalinization plants for water, but those plants can only provide 45 percent of demand, and their operation is energy heavy and produces much greenhouse gas. This activity has been used by age fourteen students in Cyprus and involves linear functions and concepts from statistics.

Classroom Context

This activity is designed for four forty-minute sessions. The first session deals with background information and readiness questions with an introduction to Google Earth if needed. The final three sessions are for modeling and solving the problem and for documenting the results. Students work in groups of three to four to solve the problem, but document their results by writing an individual letter to the Water Management Board.

Teacher Notes

A teacher may have students consider newspaper articles and quotations such as the following. Alex Chris, a landscape gardener, said many of the water boreholes in Nicosia, Cyprus's capital, are now pumping mud. "I installed one expensive garden with 500 m of irrigation pipe in Nicosia a few months ago," he said. "Last week they called to tell me the system had stopped, and their trees and lawns were dying. I found that sludge had been pumped through the pipes."

Additionally, last week people all over Cyprus received a water conservation advisory via mail. In that advisory, the head of the Cyprus Water Board talked about the island's reliance on desalinization plants saying, "We don't desalinate lightly, without being aware of the consequences. It is energy-consuming…and this causes [greenhouse gas] emissions for which Cyprus has to pay fines." Cypriot officials recently decided to sign a contract with a nearby country to import more than twelve million cubic meters of water over the summer, starting at the end of June. Officials will also sign a contract with a shipping company to use oil tankers for supplying Cyprus with water.

After students read the newspaper reports, the teacher may choose to ask the following three questions that may entail some Google Earth research. After these questions, the students may begin work on the problem in groups of three or four.

1. Who is Alex Chris?

2. How many desalination plants for water are currently in Cyprus? Why does the Cyprus government not build more desalination plants?

3. Which solution did the Water Board decide to adopt for solving the water problem?

Before students begin the decision making in this project, the teacher may wish to discuss qualitative and quantitative information, the importance of each, and have a full class discussion for how qualitative measures may be used.

Extensions

As an extension of this activity, students might consider a comparable problem involving California's obtaining water from Alaska and Washington.

Research Notes

The activity design follows the guidelines for designing model-eliciting activities proposed by Lesh and Doerr (2003). Some background information and ideas on how students solved the water activity problem appeared in a recent publication by English and Mousoulides (2011). Further, an extended version of the activity served as the basis of a project-based task, developed within Compass, a research project that received funding from the European Commission (www.compass-project.eu).

In the *Common Core State Standards for Mathematics* in the United States, modeling with mathematics is one of the practices for all grade levels: "Mathematically proficient students can apply the mathematics they know to solve problems arising in everyday life, society, and the work place....Mathematically proficient students who can apply what they know are comfortable making assumptions and approximations to simplify a complicated situation, realizing that these may need revision later. They are able to identify important quantities in a practical situation and map their relationships using such tools as diagrams, two-way tables, graphs, flowcharts, and formulas. They can analyze those relationships mathematically to draw conclusions" (National Governors Association Center for Best Practices [NGA Center] and Council of Chief State School Officers [CCSSO] 2010, p. 7).

REFERENCES

English, Lyn, and Nicholas Mousoulides. "Engineering-based Modelling Experiences in the Elementary Classroom." In *Dynamic Modeling: Cognitive Tool for Scientific Inquiry,* edited by Myint Swe Khine and Issa M. Saleh, pp. 173–94. New York: Springer, 2011.

Lesh, Richard, and Helen Doerr. *Beyond Constructivism: A Models and Modeling Perspective on Mathematics Problem Solving, Learning and Teaching.* Mahwah, N.J.: Lawrence Erlbaum Associates, 2003.

National Governors Association Center for Best Practices and Council of Chief State School Officers (NGA Center and CCSSO). *Common Core State Standards for Mathematics.* Washington, D.C.: NGA Center and CCSSO, 2010. http://www.corestandards.org.

Activity Sheet

Consider the following newspaper articles and quotations from the Cypriot press. Alex Chris, a landscape gardener, said many of the water boreholes in Nicosia, Cyprus's capital, are now pumping mud. "I installed one expensive garden with 500 m of irrigation pipe in Nicosia a few months ago," he said. "Last week they called to tell me the system had stopped, and their trees and lawns were dying. I found that sludge had been pumped through the pipes."

Additionally, last week people all over Cyprus received a water conservation advisory via mail. In that advisory, the head of the Cyprus Water Board talked about the island's reliance on desalinization plants, saying, "We don't desalinate lightly, without being aware of the consequences. It is energy-consuming...and this causes [greenhouse gas] emissions for which Cyprus has to pay fines." Cypriot officials recently decided to sign a contract with a nearby country to import more than twelve million cubic meters of water over the summer, starting at the end of June. Officials will also sign a contract with a shipping company to use oil tankers for supplying Cyprus with water.

The Cyprus Water Board must decide from which country Cyprus will import water for the next summer period. Lebanon, Greece, Syria, and Egypt each expressed a willingness to supply Cyprus with water. The Water Board received information in the table below about the water price in euros, how much water each country can supply Cyprus with during summer, oil tanker cost for transportation, and port facilities for the tankers.

Country	Water supply per week (metric tons)	Water price (metric ton)	Tanker capacity (metric tons)	Tanker oil cost per 100 km	Port facilities for tankers
Egypt	3 000 000	€ 4.00	30 000	€ 20 000	Average
Greece	4 000 000	€ 2.00	50 000	€ 25 000	Very Good
Lebanon	2 000 000	€ 5.20	30 000	€ 20 000	Average
Syria	3 000 000	€ 5.00	30 000	€ 20 000	Good

Note: € is the symbol for euro.

Using the information provided, you are to assist the Board in making the best possible choice. Write a letter to the Board explaining your reasoning for the recommendation you make. Carefully outline your method so that the Board might use your method for making similar decisions in the future.

Hint: You may need to use Google Earth to explore the major ports in the various countries, draw the tanker routes for delivery, and make accurate calculations to determine costs. Your argument may also include a final estimate for how much a metric ton of water will cost if bought from each of the countries.

Note that the quality of the port facility is a qualitative measure; a decision that may have to be made is how to quantify this information to help make the choice. Additional factors may be environmental such as sea pollution, tanker oil use, and so forth.